ACTION RESEARCH
SECOND EDITION

To *Rosalie*, partner, lover, friend, and colleague,
whose love sustains me.

And to *Simon*, *Jeremy*, and *Benjamin*, who have
shared so much of my life.

ACTION RESEARCH

SECOND EDITION

Ernest T. Stringer

SAGE Publications
International Educational and Professional Publisher
Thousand Oaks   London   New Delhi

For information:

SAGE Publications, Inc.
2455 Teller Road
Thousand Oaks, California 91320
E-mail: order@sagepub.com

SAGE Publications Ltd.
6 Bonhill Street
London EC2A 4PU
United Kingdom

SAGE Publications India Pvt. Ltd.
M-32 Market
Greater Kailash I
New Delhi 110048 India

Printed in the United States of America

Library of Congress Cataloging-in-Publication Data

Stringer, Ernest T.
    Action research / Ernest T. Stringer. — 2nd ed.
    p. cm.
    Includes bibliographical references and index.
    ISBN 0-7619-1712-8 (cloth; acid-free paper)
    ISBN 0-7619-1713-6 (pbk; acid-free paper)
    1. Human services—Research. 2. Action research. I. Title.
    HV11 .S835 1999
    361—dc21   99-6437

00 01 02 03 04 8 7 6 5 4 3 2

Acquiring Editor:	Peter Labella
Editorial Assistant:	Renée Piernot
Production Editor:	Wendy Westgate
Production Assistant:	Karen Wiley
Typesetter/Designer:	Danielle Dillahunt
Cover Designer:	Ravi Balasuriya

Contents

Foreword

I was recently asked, in another context, to speculate on the future of educational research if it were to change in directions that I personally hoped for. My response was that I hoped *all* research that might properly be called *human* inquiry would exhibit three characteristics: decentralization, deregulation, and cooperativeness in execution. I believe that this book describes a mode of inquiry that fits all these specifications.

By *decentralization,* I meant to indicate a movement away from efforts to uncover generalizable truths toward a new emphasis on local context. The hiatus between theory and practice has been remarked on too often to require rehearsal here. The reason for that hiatus, I have long asserted, lies in the gap between general laws and specific applications; such laws can have, at best, only probabilistic implications for specific cases. The fact, for example, that 80% of patients presenting a given set of symptoms are likely to have lung cancer does not imply that a particular patient with those symptoms ought immediately be rushed into surgery.

We have witnessed, during the past half century or so, determined efforts to find general solutions to social problems, be they low pupil achievement, drug abuse, alcoholism, AIDS, or other challenges. The cost to national economies has been prodigious, and there is precious little to show for it—"little bang for the buck," as some folks are wont to say. It ought to be apparent by now that generalized, one-size-fits-all solutions do not work. The devil (or God, if you prefer) is in the details. Without intimate knowledge of local context, one cannot hope to devise solutions to local problems. *All* problems are de facto local; inquiry must be decentralized to the local context.

By *deregulation*, I meant to indicate a movement away from the restrictive conventional rules of the research game, the overweening concern with validity, reliability, objectivity, and generalizability. I have argued in other contexts that these methodological criteria can have meaning only within a paradigm of inquiry that is defined in the conventional way and, specifically, based on the premise of concrete, tangible reality. However useful the premise of such a reality may be in the physical sciences (and history has shown it to be useful there indeed), it is simply irrelevant in the arena of human inquiry, because in that arena there is no tangible reality; everything that social inquirers study depends on mental constructions, mental interpretations. Thus the usual distinction between ontology (the nature of reality) and epistemology (how one comes to know that reality) collapses: Inquirers do not discover knowledge by watching nature do its thing from behind a thick one-way mirror; rather, it is literally created by the interaction of inquirers with the object (construct) inquired into. Whatever the criteria for research quality may be in this new arena, the conventional criteria clearly are not they.

By *cooperativeness in execution*, I meant to indicate a style of inquiry in which there is no functional distinction between the researcher and the researched (*subjects*, in conventional parlance). They are all defined as participants, and they all have equal footing in determining what questions will be asked, what information will be analyzed, and how conclusions and courses of action will be determined. These partici-pants, sometimes called *stakeholders* or *local members,* may include some with special training in inquiry, but if so, these specialists have no privilege in determining how the study will go; all participants share the perquisites of privilege. I insist on this joint approach both because local stakeholders are the only extant experts on local culture, beliefs, and practices and because moral considerations require that local per-spectives be honored.

The reader will quickly see, I am sure, that this book conforms to these stipulations exceptionally well. On the matter of decentralization,

Dr. Stringer takes issue with "applied scientific expertise" aimed at "eradicat[ing] [a] problem by applying some intervention at an individual or programmatic level" (Chapter 1). He argues that "evidence suggests that centralized policies and programs generated by 'experts' have limited success" in overcoming problems. His proposal for *community-based* action research returns the focus of inquiry to the local context.

On the matter of deregulation, Dr. Stringer asserts that

> formal research operates at a distance from the everyday lives of practitioners, and . . . largely fails to penetrate the experienced reality of their day-to-day work. The objective and generalizable knowledge embodied in social and behavioral research often is irrelevant to the conflicts [they] encounter. (Chapter 1)

He opts instead for the resurgence of action research, which is fundamentally different from the classic approach of defining variables and generating therefrom, through hypotheses and tests, explanations for why people behave as they do. That action research may not conform to conventional criteria of research rigor is much less important than that it takes a more democratic, empowering, and humanizing approach; assists locals in extending their own understanding of their situations; and helps them to resolve the problems they see as important.

On the matter of cooperativeness in execution, Dr. Stringer calls for a form of inquiry that represents a "moral intertwining" of all participants, including, of course, the inquirer. The major concerns that occupy the attention of all but the most ardently conservative investigators—empowerment, democracy, equity, liberation, freedom from oppression, and life enhancement—are central to community-based action research. Ethics and morality are inscribed as essential features of human inquiry—not simply as standards to be met in the interest of humanity but as standards that determine the very nature of study outcomes. Values cannot be separated from the core of an inquiry by the simple expedient of claiming objectivity, because findings are literally created by the inquiry process. And that process is permeated by values at every step.

Now, all of this has a very theoretical sound, and that lack of grounding is one of the major difficulties that has accompanied various calls for new approaches, new paradigms. However important theoretical justifications may be, they have little value if their implications are not translated into forms useful to the *practitioners* of this nontraditional social research. It is this urgent need to which this book responds, and, in my opinion, responds very well. Let me mention several of its features that commend it for this purpose:

- The language of the book is eminently accessible to practitioners who may be unfamiliar with typical research parlance. This is clearly not a book written solely for professional researchers; it is within the grasp of any reasonably literate reader. There is no arcane language to confuse the unwary.

- Every procedure described is accompanied by step-by-step instructions. The professional researcher may find these instructions unnecessarily detailed, but the novice will surely appreciate being helped at each juncture. And even the professional will find the details useful precisely because the approach differs so dramatically from what is normally found in a research methods text.

- The book is written to be useful to a wide variety of audiences, including but not limited to teachers, health workers, social workers, community workers, counselors, and many other lay workers and professionals. But to say that a book is intended to be useful for this or that audience has little meaning unless those audience members can find themselves represented in examples and depicted in situations. This aim is well met in this volume.

- The representations made by the author are illustrated throughout by personal anecdotes. Indeed, the inclusion of these anecdotes is perhaps the most useful feature of the book, because it makes clear to the reader that the author is speaking from a wealth of personal experience. He has not only "talked the talk" but also "walked the walk." The reader can have confidence that every assertion has been validated in a real-life situation and that every procedure recommended has been found to work in some real-life instance. And precisely because the author makes plain that his background is not essentially dissimilar from the reader's, the reader will find these anecdotes confidence building. What is proposed is not only possible for an expert but also possible for an everyday reader as well. And if it can work with a cultural group as different as that of the Australian Aboriginal, it can probably work in just about any cultural setting.

It is not only the practitioner of community-based action research with whom Dr. Stringer is concerned, however; he is equally interested in persuading the more conservative academic of the soundness of his proposals. Accordingly, he includes a final chapter that sets the whole in a proper theoretical context. Here he reviews and reflects on the material presented in the earlier, more practical chapters, as he says, to "[test] it . . . against the reality of our everyday experience." His reflections address the question of the legitimacy of his proposed approach, to secure for it a wider acceptance, discuss the issues of power and control, and set action research in the context of the postmodern position. The skeptic and the critic may or may not find his arguments persuasive, but, if taken seriously, they raise important questions about which each reader will have to satisfy him- or herself. The novice may take comfort in that rational arguments do exist for the practice of a type of inquiry that many practitioners have intuitively felt to be right (for them) but about which they have felt insecure on the grounds of rigor or objectivity. There is indeed more in heaven and earth than has been dreamed of in the received philosophy.

EGON G. GUBA

Preface

The Purpose of This Book

This book has been written for those workers, both professional and nonprofessional, who provide services to people in community, organizational, or institutional contexts. It speaks, therefore, to teachers, health workers, social workers, community and youth workers, planners, and a whole range of other people who function in teaching, service delivery, or managerial roles. Its purpose is to provide a set of research tools that will enable these individuals to deal effectively with many of the problems that confront them as they enact their work.

This volume also provides guidance to that increasing body of scholars and students engaging in research in university settings. Until recently, academic research was the province of highly trained technicians who engaged in research designed to speak to the underlying dynamics of social life. Using sophisticated experimental and statistical techniques, they sought to define the fundamental mechanisms that defined social life. Recent developments in thought related to naturalistic, qualitative, and interpretive inquiry have opened the door for a much broader array of research, making possible more localized research that speaks to the issues of professional practitioners in training.

Although this volume is presented as a handbook for practitioners, it has a more serious intent. It represents an approach to research that takes seriously the critiques of traditional research methodologies that are inherent in postmodern, feminist, and critical theory. Community-based action research is presented, therefore, as a reemerging tradition that links processes of inquiry to the lives of people as they come to grips with the problems and stresses that beset them in their day-to-day lives.

The Genesis of Action Research

As I reviewed the literature in preparation for writing this book, I read a number of interpretations of the genesis of action research, all of them interesting and informative, but all citing different authors and providing quite disparate histories. Readers who are interested in examples of this diversity should follow the different routes to interpreting action research provided by Kemmis and McTaggart (1988); Anderson, Herr, and Nihlen (1994); and Reason (1994). The common themes that emerge from these authors provide the glue that enables us to link their interpretations with this book. They all acknowledge fundamental investment in processes that

- Are rigorously empirical and reflective (or interpretive)
- Engage people who have traditionally been called *subjects* as active participants in the research process
- Result in some practical outcome related to the lives or work of the participants

Community-based action research sits comfortably with these agendas but has an added dimension that relates to the hidden curriculum of most social encounters. That is, it is designed to encourage an approach to research that potentially has both practical and theoretical outcomes but that does so in ways that provide conditions for continuing action— the formation of a sense of community.

Action research has links to and is informed by a variety of intellectual traditions, although it is not defined by any one of them. Operationally, it is usual to acknowledge the seminal work of Kurt Lewin (1946) and, more recently, Carr and Kemmis (1986) and Reason and Rowan (1981). Action research has much in common, however, with a range of other traditions, including practitioner research, action inquiry, action science, and community development. Its intellectual roots are likewise diverse; action research has been linked to Moreno (1956), Freire (1974), and the critical theory associated with Habermas (1979) and the Frankfurt school.

The Style of This Book

In keeping with the underlying principles of the traditions described above, therefore, I present this book on community-based action research in ways that make it most accessible to the practitioner. The volume's voice, style, and orientation are directed to teachers, health workers, social workers, community workers, administrators, and other human service workers and speak to their professional agendas. I attempt to provide clear guidelines to enable novice practitioner researchers to move comfortably through a process of inquiry that provides effective solutions to significant problems in their work lives. The "biographical bulletins" that punctuate the text are designed to clarify meaning and to increase understanding of relevant facets of research processes.

The Role of the Researcher

When I commenced this book, I wrote directly to the practitioner researcher as the person who would enact his or her own research processes. I soon realized, however, that community-based action research involves a number of groups whose activities must be facilitated or coordinated by an individual or a small group of researchers. The task of the practitioner researcher is to provide leadership and direction to other participants or stakeholders in the research process. I therefore speak throughout this book to those who coordinate or facilitate the research as *research facilitators*. For ease and clarity, I often shorten this to *researchers* or *facilitators*. Practitioners may accept the role of researcher, therefore, when they enact research processes with groups of other stakeholders—students, clients, administrators, and so on. All participants in the research process, however, should rightfully be called researchers.

In many situations, the demands of professional or community life prevent practitioners from taking such an active leadership role, and they may call on the services of outside consultants to perform coordinating, facilitating functions. In such cases, therefore, the consultants would accept the role designated in this book as researchers or research facilitators.

Structure of the Book

This book is intended to be a resource for practitioners, to assist them in their efforts to conduct inquiry, and to hone their investigative skills so that they might formulate effective solutions to the deep-rooted problems that detract from the quality of their professional lives. In the chapters that follow, I present an approach to inquiry that will help practitioners explore systematically the real-life problems they experience in their work contexts and formulate effective and sustainable solutions that will enhance the lives of the people they serve.

Chapter 1 reviews the nature of research and provides an overview of community-based action research. It includes a discussion of the values inherent in this approach to research—empowerment, democracy, equity, liberation, and life enhancement—and suggestions concerning professional, organizational, and community contexts in which action research might be appropriately applied.

Chapter 2 presents an overview of the methodology of community-based action research and a simple routine—look, think, act—that serves as a framework to guide the research process. It also provides a clear description of the role of the researcher and the principles that guide the enactment of this type of research. Unlike the objective approach of traditional scientific research, community-based action research overtly engages the human relationships that are involved, is concerned with the style and manner of communication among people, and purposefully includes all those affected by the research as active participants in the process.

Chapter 3 presents the preliminary activity required to ensure that research processes are set effectively in their community contexts. The discussion includes suggestions of ways for researchers to establish initial contact with people in a community and appropriate roles for those facilitating the research process, procedures for developing a network of contacts, and processes for constructing a preliminary understanding of the context in which the research will take place.

Chapter 4 addresses the first stage of the research process, including discussion of ways of gathering information such as observation, interviews, and document searches and the processes through which participants clearly formulate a collective description of their context.

Chapter 5 provides a description of the process through which stakeholders interpret or analyze their situations to construct joint explanations and extend their understanding of what is happening. The chapter begins with a brief discussion of the purpose of interpretive work, then presents a set of procedures for developing interpretive accounts or explanations. The final section of the chapter provides a selection of activities that can be incorporated into these procedures.

Chapter 6 presents procedures that enable participants to formulate practical solutions to their problems. Three phases of activity are described: planning, in which priorities are set and tasks defined; implementing, the supporting, modeling, and linking activity that enables participants to accomplish their tasks; and evaluating, through which participants review their progress.

Chapter 7 focuses on more complex contexts, in which practitioners engage the difficult issues and deep-seated problems often contained within large organizations, government agencies, business corporations, and some community contexts. The chapter first focuses on planning and organizational arrangements that help participants maintain the control and direction of their activities and then provides an orientation to organization and management, long-term planning processes, organizational arrangements for implementing activities, and evaluation procedures.

Chapter 8 suggests ways of organizing and formulating formal reports. It contrasts ways of structuring experimental scientific reports with structures appropriate for interpretive action research, then presents a more detailed approach to formulation of the latter. Although this style of reporting is relevant to formal reports required in bureaucratic settings and funding agencies, it is particularly suited to academic reports required for university theses and dissertations.

The final chapter reviews and reflects on the research processes presented in the book. Here I address the question of the legitimacy of community-based action research and provide a discussion of how I make sense of this approach to inquiry with reference to the perspectives of postmodern social theory. I also address some of the more recent issues in the theoretical literature related to "giving voice" to the people in emerging experimental approaches to interpretive research. The overall intent is to extend the readers' understanding of the nature of the research processes in which they participate.

The Second Edition

The second edition emerges from my experience in university contexts during the past few years. Although the first edition, based on my work in community contexts in the previous decade, provided material that has proved eminently suited to emerging directions in academic research, faculty and students struggled to find ways to fit the "look, think, act" processes to the formal requirements of university settings and funding authorities. The second edition provides material that not only clarifies and extends some of the ideas presented in the first edition but also includes a new chapter derived from attempts to formulate research processes in ways that made sense in university and bureaucratic settings.

In seeking to clarify the research processes, I have also included boxed summaries at the end of each chapter. These may be used as checklists, enabling research participants and facilitators to ensure that they work systematically through the processes of investigation and inquiry.

Finally, I have included an appendix that provides an entry into the increasingly important world of electronic resources. During the past few years, I have engaged in numerous conversations with people who participate in the Action Research List (ARLIST), which not only provides interesting ideas but also extends the resources that are now available internationally. Our world is shrinking.

Acknowledgments

When a book is written, it is customary for the author to acknowledge the contributions of those who have assisted in its development. I would like to explore the nature of those contributions, because they go much further, I believe, than is customarily acknowledged. As I wrote this book, I became increasingly aware how little of it was my own, in any fundamental sense—how little of it was new or unique or the result of my unassisted labors. The more I read and talked with others, the more I became aware that much of what I had to say had been written or said before. The notion of intellectual property, with its implicit concept of ownership, is difficult to contemplate in such circumstances. If this book has anything new or unique, it is that particular way in which I have chosen to present the ideas it contains. All else is taken, borrowed, or copied, either consciously or unconsciously, from people with whom I have worked or whose works I have read.

Nevertheless, I can name some of the sources from which my ideas emanate. Community development workers in Western Australia, with whom I worked for many years, provided many of the basic ideas from which this book is derived. An incomplete list includes Fran Crawford, Bill Genat, Rosalie Dwyer, Tony McMahon, Rod Mitchell, and Sue Young. The person with whom I served an illuminative field apprenticeship was Doug McCauley, a good friend who provided me with much on-the-ground experience and the basic practice frameworks from which mine have evolved. These frameworks have been enriched immeasurably, initially by Russell Gluck and then, through the years, by another good friend, Tony Kelly, who continues to enhance the work of practitioners across Australia.

Throughout this time, my understanding of the application of frameworks and practices was constantly strengthened and transformed in my interactions with Aboriginal colleagues Darryl Kickett, Trevor Satour, Carol Martin, David Corbett, Darlene Oxenham, and Glenis Grogan. I am also conscious of the challenges provided by Pat Dudgeon, until recently the head of the Centre for Aboriginal Studies, and the particular support, in recent years, of the coordinator of postgraduate studies, Jill Abdullah.

My progression from community development to action research came during my 2-year stay at the College of Education at Texas A&M University. Jim Kracht, then head of the Department of Educational Curriculum and Instruction, provided me with the opportunity to enter a rich intellectual environment that included Professors Yvonna Lincoln, Pat Larke, and Carolyn Clark. The students in my classes at this time engaged in the exploration and development of ideas that were eventually synthesized in this book. The enthusiasm and challenges provided by Mary Frances Agnello, Shelia Baldwin, Alice Buchanan, Lois Christensen, Deana and Kenneth Henry, Patti Nason, Vicki Newman, Terresa Katt Payne, Rhonda Petty, Kathryn Powell, Patsy Tinsley, and many others both encouraged and stimulated the development of ideas that have emerged in this work. I am also grateful for Ann Alsmeyer's editorial assistance, which enabled me to upgrade my writing skills significantly and enhanced the technical quality of the manuscript.

It was Egon Guba, however, who provided the impetus for me to write this book. I visited Egon initially to grapple with some of the deeper philosophical issues that were emerging from the class in community-based ethnography that I was teaching at the time. As we engaged in dialogue, he first hinted, then encouraged, then prodded me to express my ideas as a coherent work. Few people have the opportunity to engage in continued dialogue with and to have the intellectual and experiential support of a person such as Egon. I feel myself privileged to have had that opportunity and relish the memory of the afternoons I spent in his comfortable lounge room exploring ideas or listening to his feedback on the individual chapters as they were written. I thank him for that delightful, life-enhancing experience, which invigorated my thinking and provided the intellectual energy for this book.

My partner, wife, companion, and friend, Rosalie Dwyer, lived with me through the long period from gestation to completion of the first edition of the book. Her thoughtful comments, active encouragement, detailed scrutiny, and constant companionship provided the personal and spiritual energy that sustained me through the arduous and repetitive process of writing and editing.

I would also like to acknowledge the many friends, colleagues, and students who, by engaging in more recent discussions, have caused me to reconsider or clarify many of the ideas presented in this second edition. They include, particularly, those who met in dinner/discussion groups in homes around the Fremantle area, and Don Zancanella, Penny Pence, and Betsy Noll at the University of New Mexico, where I spent a productive fall semester in 1998. Penny Pence provided invaluable assistance in preparing the second edition and the clarity of the new material can be attributed to her sharp and creative editorial skills. Finally, I would like to acknowledge Peter Labella, who signed me for the first edition, worked with me through the stages of production, and suggested that I prepare this second edition. These friends and colleagues enrich the work in which I engage. I thank them all.

ERNIE STRINGER

Research in Professional and Public Life

For many people, professional and service occupations such as teaching, social work, health care, and other forms of public service provide appealing avenues of employment. Regular work, reasonable salaries, and comfortable working conditions complement interesting and fulfilling work that includes the potential for exploration of a variety of career opportunities. Increasingly, however, people in these sectors find their work to be more demanding and less satisfying. They often struggle to balance growing demands on their time and energy as workloads continue to expand, and they are routinely confronted by problems rarely encountered 20 or 30 years ago.

The pressures experienced in professional practice reflect tensions that exist in modern society. The complex influences that impinge on people's everyday social lives provide a fertile seedbed for a proliferating host of family, community, and institutional problems. Professional practitioners and agency workers are increasingly held accountable for solutions to problems that have their roots in the deeply complex interaction between the experiences of individual people and the realities of their social lives: stress, unemployment, family breakdown, alienation, behavioral problems, violence, poverty, discrimination, conflict, and so on.

Although adequately prepared to deal with the technical requirements of their daily work, practitioners face recurrent crises that are outside the scope of their professional expertise. Teachers face children disturbed by conflict in their homes and communities, youth workers encounter resentful and alienated teenagers, health workers confront people apparently unconcerned about life-threatening lifestyles and social habits, and social and welfare workers are strained past their capacity to deal with the impossible caseloads spawned by increasing poverty and alienation.

There is an expectation in social life that trained professionals, applying scientifically derived expertise, will provide answers to the proliferating problems that confront people in their personal and public lives. Community responses to crises that arise from drug abuse, crime, violence, school absenteeism, and so on invariably revolve around the use of a social worker, a youth worker, a counselor, or similar type of service provider whose task it is to eradicate the problem by applying some intervention at an individual or programmatic level. These responses have failed to diminish the growing social problems that have multiplied much faster than the human and financial resources available to deal with them. Moreover, evidence suggests that centralized policies and programs generated by "experts" have limited success in resolving these problems. The billions of dollars invested in social programs have failed to stem the tide of alienation and disaffection that characterizes social life in modern industrial nations.

If there are answers to these proliferating social problems, it is likely that centralized policies will need to be complemented by the creative action of those who are closest to their sources—the service professionals, agency workers, students, clients, communities, and families who face the issues on a daily basis. Centralized policies, programs, and services, I suggest, should allow practitioners to engage the human potential of all people who contribute to the lives of the specific contexts in which they work. Policies and programs should not dictate specific actions and procedures but should provide the resources to enable appropriate action to be taken.

The daily work of practitioners often involves face-to-face contact with many community groups. This interaction provides many opportunities for practitioners to acquire valuable insights into people's social worlds and to assist them in formulating effective solutions to problems that permeate their lives. Unfortunately, the technical skills that professionals acquire in their training are usually inadequate to provide practitioners with the means to work at this level. Other capacities are required.

Industry has long recognized the need to maintain the skill levels of the workforce. Companies in the commercial and business world usually invest significant proportions of their budgets in human resources development, to ensure that their workers have the skills and knowledge necessary to keep them abreast of new techniques, technologies, and conditions. The need is just as clear in public and professional life. Service practitioners should strive to cultivate the skills that will help them investigate and master systematically the issues affecting them and their constituencies.

In this process, we must change our vision of social service workers and administrators from one of professional as mechanic/technician to one of professional as creative investigator and problem solver. This new vision rejects the mindless application of standardized practices across all settings and contexts and instead advocates the use of contextually relevant procedures formulated by inquiring and resourceful practitioners.

People in many arenas have already begun to enact this way of viewing their work. Centralized bureaucracies are under increasing pressure to devolve their decision-making power, and participatory approaches to management likewise are transforming the operations of many companies in the commercial and business world. This changing consciousness signals a move away from centralized procedures and processes and gives notice of the need to extend the developmental capabilities of practitioners.

This book is intended as a resource for those practitioners who wish to take advantage of these new movements in community, institutional, and organizational life. In the pages that follow, I describe some of the ways they can hone their investigative skills, engage in systematic approaches to inquiry, and formulate effective and sustainable solutions to the deep-rooted problems that diminish the quality of professional life. This volume presents an approach to inquiry that seeks not only to enrich professional practice but also to enhance the lives of those involved.

As a young teacher, I had the rare experience of being transferred from the relative security of a suburban classroom to a primary school in a remote desert region of Western Australia.[1] My task was to provide "education" for the children of the traditional hunter-gatherer Aboriginal people who lived in that area. On my first day in class, I was confronted by a wall of silence that effectively prevented any possibility of teaching. The children refused to respond verbally to any of my queries or comments, hanging their heads, averting their eyes, and sometimes responding so softly that I was unable to hear what they said. In these discomfiting circumstances, I was unable to work through any of the customary routines and activities that had constituted my professional repertoire in the city. Lessons were abbreviated, avuncular, and disjointed, and my professional pride took a distinct jolt as an ineffective reading lesson followed an inarticulate math period and preceded the monotony of my singular voice through social studies.

The silence of the children in the classroom was in marked contrast to their happy chatter as we walked through the surrounding bush in the afternoon, my failing spirit leading me to present an impromptu "natural science" lesson. I was eventually able to resolve many of the problems that faced me in this unique educational environment, but the experience endowed me with an inquiring professional mind. In these circumstances, all the taken-for-granted assumptions of my professional life were up for grabs as I struggled to understand the nature of the problems that confronted me and to formulate appropriate educational experiences for this wonderfully unique group of students. Texts, curricula, teaching materials, learning activities, classroom organization, speech, interactional styles, and all other facets of classroom life became subjects of inquiry and investigation as I sought to resolve the constant stream of issues and problems that emerged in this environment. To be an effective teacher, I discovered that it was necessary to modify and adapt my regular professional routines and practices to fit the children's cultural realities.

The legacy of that experience has remained with me. Even as I later lived and taught in Texas, my inquiring eye turned to the pedagogical issues involved in the classes that I taught. Teaching has become, for me, not only a set of routines and practices but also a set of general problems, the resolution of which becomes the focus of my professional investigation. The general types of questions with which I commence—What should I teach? How can this be learned? How can I organize the learning?—are complemented by more specific queries that arise in the processes of my classes—Why are students having difficulty with this piece of work? Why does this small group of students appear disinterested in their learning? How can I deal with the few students who are unengaged and appear intent on disrupting my carefully formulated teaching/learning processes? My inquiring mind engages, examines, explores, formulates answers, and devises responses designed to overcome the educational problems that confront me.

In this situation, I now cast myself as teacher-researcher, so that research has become a continuing part of my professional life. The investigative tools that I have acquired in my academic life not only are useful for broader investigations but also provide techniques and procedures that can be fruitfully applied to my day-to-day work in schools, organizations, and community settings.

Research: Methodical Processes of Inquiry

Research is systematic and rigorous inquiry or investigation that enables people to understand the nature of problematic events or phenomena. Research can be characterized by the following:

- A *problem* to be investigated
- A *process of inquiry*
- *Explanations* that enable individuals to understand the nature of the problem

Research can also incorporate actions that attempt to resolve the problem being investigated.

Research can be visualized as nothing more than a natural extension of the activities in which we engage every day of our lives. Even for simple problems—Where are my blue socks? Why did the cake burn?—we ask questions that lead to explanations that provide the basis for solutions (I wore my blue socks yesterday; I probably put them with the laundry. The oven seemed hot, or maybe I left the cake in the oven longer than I should). Tentative explanations (hypotheses) may lead us to increase the information available to work toward a suggested resolution to the problem that may then be tested (I looked in the laundry, and the socks were there. Next time I baked the cake, I lowered the temperature of the oven and did not burn the cake).

The success of scientific research can be ascribed to its insistence on precise and rigorous formulation of description, observation, and explanation. The meticulous association of what is observed and what is explained provides explanations whose power and efficacy enable us to predict and control many facets of the physical world. The success of a scientific approach to research is embodied in the technical achievements that continue to transform our modern world.

Less successful, however, have been the attempts of the social and behavioral sciences to emulate the accomplishments of the physical sciences. Despite a profusion of theory, the application of scientific method to human events has failed to provide a means for predicting and controlling individual or social behavior. Teachers, health workers, and human service practitioners often find that the theoretical knowledge of the academic world has limited relevance to the exacting demands of their everyday professional lives.

This state of affairs is at least partly a function of the ways in which research traditionally has been envisaged. Formal research operates at a distance from the everyday lives of practitioners, and, although it provides interesting theoretical perspectives about the nature and complexities of social life, it largely fails to penetrate the experienced reality of their day-to-day work. The objective and generalizable knowledge embodied in social and behavioral research often is irrelevant to the conflicts that practitioners encounter or has little impact on the difficulties they face.

Pressures have emerged, therefore, for approaches to research that are more directly relevant to the work of practitioners. In recent decades, new research paradigms, variously labeled *qualitative, naturalistic, constructivist,* and *interpretivist,* have sought to provide researchers with new ways to understand the nature of the social world. These paradigms have pursued an interpretive task that seeks to describe the historic, cultural, and interactional complexity of social life. In doing so, they endeavor to develop accounts that more fully represent people's lived experiences. Explanations are derived from the ordinary understandings—folk theories—at work in any cultural context and the everyday behaviors and social processes that surround and shape people's lives.

Even these explanations have their limitations, however, because they fail to provide any essential link between theory and practice. Understanding the nature of the social and cultural context often is useful and interesting but, once again, fails to connect with the everyday world of the practitioner. General explanations do not often provide the means to change work practices.

More recently, therefore, we have witnessed the reemergence of a tradition that carries this process a step further. Action research is based on the assumption that the mere recording of events and formulation of explanations by an uninvolved researcher is inadequate in and of itself. A further assumption is that those who have previously been designated as "subjects" should participate directly in research processes and that those processes should be applied in ways that benefit all participants directly. Community-based action research is a derivative of this approach to inquiry.

As a graduate student, I was excited by the possibilities of the hypotheticodeductive method of research. Here, I thought, was the means for obtaining answers to the significant social problems that concerned me. By careful measurement of critical variables related to the problem under investigation and precise definition and measurement of the relationship between them, it would be possible to describe the genesis of the problem and take appropriate steps to resolve it. The major task was simply to identify the appropriate variables, measure them, and analyze them using appropriate statistical techniques. It would then be possible to predict the ways people would behave or perform in particular circumstances and to take remedial action.

In my attempts to understand the reason for low achievement levels of minority students, I set out to map the variables that had impacts on their school performance, with the intent of first defining, then measuring, the extent of the relationships between the factors that related to their academic performance. I equipped myself for the task by taking many courses in descriptive and inferential statistics and experimental and survey research methods, while concomitantly immersing myself in the voluminous and burgeoning research literature that spoke to these issues.

My disenchantment with this approach to inquiry came through courses in anthropology and sociology, which awakened me to a relativistic social universe. It was a perspective that revealed a world far different from the mechanistic, soulless vision that, at that time, was favored by scientists. For me, the new paradigm encompassed social spheres composed of the changing lives of people as they created and re-created their realities according to meaning systems inherent in their differing situations. The social world, I discovered, was not static and mechanistic but dynamic and changing, encapsulated by and redefined continuously by the symbolic systems of thought and language through which human beings fashion their physical and social universe.

The transformation of my thought was dramatic. I realized that I, as impartial, objective observer, could never hope to define, discover, or measure the worlds of meaning that embodied human behavior in any social setting; that any hypothesis or explanation that I formulated at a distance from those worlds of meanings could bear little meaningful relationship to the actions and activities of the people who inhabited them; and that any interpretation of their behavior that failed to take into account the ways in which participants defined and described their situations must necessarily fail as an explanatory system.

This realization was an epiphanic experience. Through rigorous exploration and inquiry, I had acquired a new vision of the world, a new way of comprehending the complexity that surrounded me, and, in doing so, reconfigured my relationship with the people I proposed to study. Far from defining and describing the variables that explained the nature of their existence and generating explanations about why they behaved as they did, I was now cast in a position of ignorance in relation to those who had previously been potential subjects of study. Only through them, the cultural experts in their own settings, could I acquire the information that would enable me to understand how they behaved as they did. A new "researcher" emerged.

Community-Based Action Research:
Participatory Approaches to Inquiry

Historically, community-based action research is related to models of action research that sought to apply the tools of anthropology and other disciplines to the practical resolution of social problems (e.g., Goodenough, 1963; Lewin, 1946). Action research ultimately suffered a decline in favor because of its association with radical political activism in the 1960s. It has reemerged in response to both pragmatic and philosophical pressures and is now more broadly understood as "disciplined inquiry (research) which seeks focused efforts to improve the quality of people's organizational, community and family lives" (Calhoun, 1993, p. 62). Community-based action research is also allied to the recent emergence of practitioner research (e.g., Anderson et al., 1994), new paradigm research (Reason, 1988), and teacher-as-researcher (e.g., Kincheloe, 1991). The approach to research suggested by community-based action research is implied within the methodological frameworks of fourth-generation evaluation (Guba & Lincoln, 1989). Their dialogic, hermeneutic (meaning-making) approach to evaluation implies a more democratic, empowering, and humanizing approach to inquiry, which is the ideological basis for community-based action research.

There has been a resurgence in the popularity of action research, perhaps because of developments in academic thought that have taken place in recent years. A noninclusive list of recent publications includes Atweh, Weeks, and Kemmis (1998); Boyarsky and Murphy (1998); Brown and Dowling (1998); Christiansen, Goulet, Krentz, and Maeers (1997); Fals-Borda and Rahman (1991); Greenwood and Levin (1998); Hart and Bond (1995); Krulfeld, MacDonald, and MacDonald (1998); McNiff (1995); McTaggart (1997); Mills (in press); Mumford (1997); Schmuck (1998); Stringer (1997); Wallace (1998); and Weisbrod and Worthy (1997).

As an evolving approach to inquiry, community-based action research speaks to the current crisis of research by envisaging a collaborative approach to investigation that seeks to engage "subjects" as equal and full participants in the research process. A fundamental premise of community-based action research is that it commences with an interest in the problems of a group, a community, or an organization. Its purpose is to assist people in extending their understanding of their situation and thus in resolving problems that confront them. Put another way, community-based action research provides a model for enacting local, action-oriented approaches to inquiry, applying small-scale theorizing to specific problems in specific situations (Denzin & Lincoln, 1994).

Community-based action research is always enacted through an explicit set of social values. In modern, democratic social contexts, it is seen as a process of inquiry that has the following characteristics:

- It is *democratic,* enabling the participation of all people.
- It is *equitable,* acknowledging people's equality of worth.
- It is *liberating,* providing freedom from oppressive, debilitating conditions.
- It is *life enhancing,* enabling the expression of people's full human potential.

Community-based action research works on the assumption, therefore, that all stakeholders—those whose lives are affected by the problem under study—should be engaged in the processes of investigation. Stakeholders participate in a process of rigorous inquiry, acquiring information (collecting data) and reflecting on that information (analyzing) to transform their understanding about the nature of the problem under investigation (theorizing). This new set of understandings is then applied to plans for resolution of the problem (action), which, in turn, provides the context for testing hypotheses derived from group theorizing (evaluation).

Collaborative exploration helps practitioners, agency workers, client groups, and other stakeholding parties to develop increasingly sophisticated understandings of the problems and issues that confront them. As they rigorously explore and reflect on their situation together, they can repudiate social myths, misconceptions, and misrepresentations and formulate more constructive analyses of their situation. By sharing their diverse knowledge and experience—expert, professional, and lay—stakeholders can create solutions to their problems and, in the process, improve the quality of their community life.

The role of the research facilitator, in this context, becomes more facilitative and less directive. Knowledge acquisition/production proceeds as a collective process, engaging people who have previously been the "subjects" of research in the process of defining and redefining the corpus of understanding on which their community or organizational life is based. As they collectively investigate their own situation, stakeholders build a consensual vision of their life-world. Community-based action research results not only in a collective vision but also in a sense of community. It operates at the intellectual level as well as at social, cultural, political, and emotional levels.

Inquiry in Use

A colleague approached me after listening to my report on one of the action research projects in which I had been involved. "You know," she said, "the difference with your work is that you expect something to actually happen as a result of your activities."

My colleague's statement characterizes, for me, one of the significant differences between action research and traditional research. Traditional research projects are complete when a report has been written and presented to the contracting agency or published in an academic journal. Community-based action research can have these purely academic outcomes and may provide the basis for rich and profound theorizing and basic knowledge production, but its primary purpose is as a practical tool for solving problems experienced by people in their professional, community, or private lives. If an action research project does not *make a difference,* in a specific way, for practitioners and/or their clients, then it has failed to achieve its objectives. The analogue of hypothesis testing in action research is some form of change or development that is tested by its ability to enhance the lives of the people with whom it is engaged.

Community-based action research has been employed successfully in schools, hospitals, health clinics, community agencies, government departments, rural communities, urban and suburban organizations, churches, youth clubs, ethnic groups, extension services, and many other settings. It has been used with factory workers, agency staff, school students, youth groups, young mothers, senior citizens, poor people, persons who are unemployed, community groups, people with particular forms of disability or illness, and so on. Community-based action research processes have been successfully facilitated by welfare workers, social workers, community workers, teachers, nurses, doctors, managers and administrators, urban and community planners, and agency workers in a wide range of social contexts.

The ability of ordinary people to engage in complex organizational work usually deemed the province of professionals has been demonstrated many times. One of the most striking examples I have seen was a community school set up by an Aboriginal group in a remote region of Australia. Weary of sending their young children 150 miles away to the nearest town for schooling, members of the community asked a young teacher to assist them in developing their own school. Untrained for this specialist task, she nevertheless worked with members of the community for some months to build the school from the ground up. Together, they formulated the curriculum and timetable, acquired teaching/learning materials and equipment, secured funding, learned how to satisfy legal and bureaucratic requirements, and built a large, grass-covered hut for a school building. When this small school commenced operation, all classes were taught in the one room, with community members helping to teach academic subjects, art, music, and language. The cultural style of the classroom was distinctively Aboriginal, with children happily and busily interacting in small groups, their work supervised by community members and the non-Aboriginal teacher. It was the most successful Aboriginal school I have seen in regard to the enthusiasm and engagement of the children and the sense of energy and excitement that typified the school's operation. Most striking, however, were the sense that community members considered it to be their school and the extent to which they continued,

through an extended period, to invest their meager financial resources
and considerable time and energy in its operation.

The following chapters present a set of routines intended to provide
guidance for practitioners who wish to engage in community-based action research. Readers may use this approach to inquiry to do several
things:

- Enhance everyday work practices by
  Reviewing goals and procedures (What things are we doing, and
     how are we doing them?)
  Evaluating effectiveness (To what extent are we achieving our
     objectives? How effective is our work?)
  Planning activities and strategies (What needs to be done? How
     do we get it done?)
- Resolve specific problems and crises by
  Defining the problem
  Exploring its context
  Analyzing its component parts
  Developing strategies for its resolution
- Develop special projects and programs by
  Planning
  Implementing
  Evaluating

Health professionals, for example, may wish to investigate and remediate poor health conditions or practices with a particular community
group (e.g., smoking, drinking, low birth weight, and inappropriate medi-
cation) and to develop appropriate remedial strategies. Schoolteachers
may investigate strategies for dealing with low student achievement
levels, poor attendance, student disinterest, or disruptive behavior.
School principals may formulate programs for increasing community
participation in their schools. Welfare workers may seek to act on the
prevalence of child abuse or neglect among client groups. Community
workers may wish to develop programs and projects to deal with the

problems of neighborhood youth. All will benefit from the use of procedures that enable them to explore systematically the conditions that operate in their specific contexts and help them develop practical plans for dealing effectively with the problems that confront them.

Some of the areas in which the application of community-based action research may be fruitful, therefore, include the following:

- Education
  School development
  Curriculum development
  Evaluation
  Classroom processes
  Class projects
  Special programs
  Parent participation
  On-site management

- Health
  Infant health programs
  Drug abuse programs
  Health promotion projects
  Community health projects
  Community health services

- Social work
  Child accommodation
  Youth programs
  Parenting programs

- Organizational development
  Review
  Planning
  Change process
  Project and program development
  Training programs
  Cross-cultural programs
  Human resource development

- Planning and architecture
  - Urban planning projects
  - Community planning projects
  - Housing development projects
  - Housing needs surveys
  - Youth housing needs

- Economic development
  - Economic development projects

Note

1. Throughout this book, I use my own experiences to illustrate points made in the text. These sections ("biographical bulletins") are set off from text with a different typeface.

Principles of Community-Based Action Research

A Basic Routine

Community-based action research is a collaborative approach to *inquiry* or *investigation* that provides people with the means to take systematic *action* to resolve specific problems. This approach to research favors consensual and participatory procedures that enable people (a) to investigate systematically their problems and issues, (b) to formulate powerful and sophisticated accounts of their situations, and (c) to devise plans to deal with the problems at hand.

Community-based action research focuses on methods and techniques of inquiry that take into account people's history, culture, interactional practices, and emotional lives. Although it makes use of techniques and strategies commonly applied in the behavioral and social sciences, it is a more user-friendly approach to investigation than most. Unlike the elaborate routines of traditional scientific research, which, from the perspective of the practitioner, are often shrouded in the mists of technical language and mystified by complex statistical procedures,

17

community-based action research is presented in terms that make it accessible to both professional practitioners and laypersons.

The routines described below have their roots in procedures that have evolved in a number of areas of professional life in the United States, Europe, Africa, Asia, and Australia and that have been used in a wide range of contexts, including rural, urban, and suburban locations in factories, schools, farms, hospitals, businesses, private organizations, and public agencies. Although effective in local group, family, and community settings, they have the potential to encompass highly complex social, cultural, and political arenas and geographically dispersed locations. Community-based action research is not a panacea for all ills and does not resolve all problems, but it does provide a means for people to "get a handle" on their situations and formulate effective solutions to problems they face in their public and professional lives.

The basic community-based action research routine—look, think, act (see Box 2.1)—starts with a simple yet powerful framework and builds greater detail into procedures as the complexity of activities increases. The terms in parentheses in Box 2.1 show how the phases of the routine relate to traditional research practices.

BOX 2.1
A Basic Action Research Routine

Look	• Gather relevant information (Gather data)
	• Build a picture: Describe the situation (Define and describe)
Think	• Explore and analyze: What is happening here? (Analyze)
	• Interpret and explain: How/why are things as they are? (Theorize)
Act	• Plan (Report)
	• Implement
	• Evaluate

The "look, think, act" routine is but one of a number of ways in which action research is envisaged. Kemmis and McTaggart (1988), for instance, present action research as a spiral of activity: plan, act, observe, reflect. Different formulations of action research reflect the diverse ways in which the same set of activities may be described, although the processes they delineate are similar. There are, after all, many ways of cutting a cake.

Although the "look, think, act" routine is presented in a linear format throughout this book, it should be read as a continually recycling set of activities (see Figure 2.1). As participants work through each of the major stages, they will explore the details of their activities through a constant process of observation, reflection, and action. At the completion of each set of activities, they will review (look again), reflect (reanalyze), and re-act (modify their actions). As experience will show, action research is not a neat, orderly activity that allows participants to proceed step-by-step to the end of the process. People will find themselves working backward through the routines, repeating processes, revising procedures, rethinking interpretations, leapfrogging steps or stages, and sometimes making radical changes in direction.

In practice, therefore, action research can be a complex process. The routines presented in this book, however, can be visualized as a road map that provides guidance to those who follow this less traveled way. Although there may be many routes to a destination, and although destinations may change, participants in the journey will be able to maintain a clear idea of their location and the direction in which they are heading.

The procedures detailed below are likely to be ineffective, however, unless enacted in ways that take into account the social, cultural,

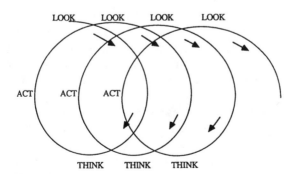

Figure 2.1. Action Research Interacting Spiral

interactional, and emotional factors that affect all human activity. "The medium is the message!" In the remainder of this chapter, therefore, I focus on some of the implicit values and underlying assumptions embedded in community-based action research. These values and assumptions are built into a set of guiding principles that can facilitate a democratic, participatory, liberating, and life-enhancing approach to research.

The Cultural Style of Action Research

Traditional approaches to research often involve an adversarial or authoritarian style that reflects the cultural ethos of competition and achievement endemic in modern societies. The scientific method itself encourages procedures that evaluate the worth of ideas by holding them up for rigorous testing and public critique. In these circumstances, the search for knowledge and understanding sometimes takes on a gladiatorial tone, as dialogue changes from inquiry to inquisition and cutting exchanges intrude into debates at conferences and in journals. Critics of traditional academic research also point to the exploitative and colonizing potential of much current research, and French scholar Michel Foucault has revealed the dynamics of power and subjugation that are inherent in the production of knowledge.

As a relatively new graduate student, I proudly presented a model that explained aspects of minority achievement to my fellow students. I had worked conscientiously on this model for many months, and although it was quite intricate, with interacting paths and parameters, it appeared to me to provide a clear and powerful way of understanding the dynamics of achievement of minority students. Having presented an outline of the model to the class, I waited for remarks, questions, or comments that would assist me in clarifying or refining the model. I was unprepared for the disparaging and dismissive response of the professor, which effectively cut off any other comment from the class and left me feeling empty and foolish, eventually escaping to the safe haven of my seat in the body of the class.

When I remember those events, I am aware of the cultural style of that dismissal: the accusatory, disdainful undertones in the voice of the professor and the embarrassed silence of my fellow students. I understand why one of the current problems of researchers is to gain entry into social settings for research purposes. I understand why professionals and laypersons alike are unwilling to have their lives and/or work scrutinized. People do not like to be judged.

Community-based action research seeks to change the social and personal dynamics of the research situation so that it is noncompetitive and nonexploitative and enhances the lives of all those who participate. This collaborative approach to inquiry seeks to build positive working relationships and productive interactional and communicative styles. Its intent is to provide a climate that enables disparate groups of people to work harmoniously and productively to achieve their various goals.

Action research has sometimes been enacted as an overtly political approach to the solution of social problems, often requiring a carefully formulated campaign to enable people to overcome their "oppressors." Although community-based research does not deny the necessity for confrontational action in some situations,[1] it is fundamentally a consensual approach to inquiry and works from the assumption that cooperation and consensus making should be the primary orientation of research activity. It seeks to link groups that potentially are in conflict so that they may attain viable, sustainable, and effective solutions to their common problems through dialogue and negotiation.

The Well-Being of the People

A key feature of community-based action research is that it takes into account the impact of activities on the lives of people engaged in or subject to investigation. Its intent is not only to "get the job done" but also to ensure the well-being of everyone involved. This notion runs contrary to many of the imperatives enshrined in bureaucratic practices that make up much of our public life. We have come to accept the impersonal, mechanistic, and allegedly objective procedures common to many health, education, and welfare services and business corporations as a necessary evil. We endure hierarchical and authoritarian modes of organization and control despite the sense of frustration, powerlessness, and stress frequently felt by both practitioners and the client groups they serve.

It is not difficult to understand the source of these frustrations. Centrally devised and controlled programs and services cannot take into account the multitude of factors that impinge on people's lives. Professional practitioners, despite their training, have only rudimentary understanding of many subtle social influences and feel compelled to implement programs and services according to formally sanctioned practices and procedures, despite their ineffectiveness in achieving the goals they were designed to accomplish. Welfare services often maintain people in states of dependency, passive and irrelevant learning processes are common in many school systems, and medical practices frequently maintain high levels of dependency on prescription drugs. All are symptomatic of underlying disorders embedded in generally accepted practices in our social institutions, agencies, and organizations.

In my professional life, I have often seen programs that isolate people from their families or communities. I have seen services that demean the recipients and organizations and agencies that operate according to rules and regulations that are shamelessly insensitive to the cultures of their clients.

I have seen young children isolated from their families for months, sometimes years at a time, that they be given a "good education." I have seen police fail to act on violence against women because the women were drunk. I have seen children taken from their home because of their parents' absence, despite the adequate care provided by their extended family. I have seen millions of dollars wasted on training programs that were purportedly designed to serve community needs but that failed to reach the people for whom they were formulated. I have seen health clinics that were incapable of caring for rural community needs because they operated according to practices common in city hospitals.

In one community, I was shown the boys' and girls' hostels for high school children, isolated from each other by the length of the town, with the girls' hostel protected by a barbed wire fence. The administrator who showed me these institutions was proud that "we haven't had an illegitimate pregnancy in years" and seemed unaware of the potential for enormous damage to family and cultural life inherent in the situation.

The list goes on and on, reflecting the failure of centrally controlled social, educational, health, welfare, and community services to adapt and adjust their operations to the social, cultural, and political realities of the specific locations where they operated. I grieve for the people who have been damaged in the process, including those workers who have become hardened to the plight of the client groups they serve.

I have seen other situations, however, in which workers have engaged the energy and potential of their constituencies and, in the process, developed programs, projects, and services with deep-seated and substantial impacts. I have seen women's groups that provided for significant needs within their communities, police initiatives that greatly enhanced the peacekeeping mission of the department, and health programs that greatly reduced the incidence of trachoma. I have also seen education and training programs traditionally shunned by minority groups later become so successful that they were unable to accommodate the numbers of people requesting entry. I have also applauded community youth programs that were able to unite hostile community factions to diminish the problems of young people in their town. I rejoice in them. They have in common a developmental process that maximized the participation of the people they served.

I have written elsewhere of the success of an independent school started by the community in which it operated. It stands in stark contrast to another school I visited. The principal, hired by an outside agency, proudly related the story of the new high school he had set up. With little assistance, he had organized the renovation of the school building, bought the furniture and equipment, designed the curriculum, and hired the teachers. "I have only one major problem," he confided. "I can't get the parents to show any interest."

As practitioners develop programs and services, therefore, or seek to solve problems that threaten the efficacy of services for which we are responsible, we need to take into account the impacts of those developments and solutions on the lives of the people we serve. Tony Kelly and

Russell Gluck (1979) propose that programs be evaluated not only according to their technical or functional worth but also according to their impacts on people's social and emotional lives. Their evaluative criteria require us to investigate the effects of our research activities on the following:

- *Pride:* people's feelings of self-worth
- *Dignity:* people's feelings of autonomy, independence, and competence
- *Identity:* people's affirmation of social identities (woman, worker, Hispanic, etc.)
- *Control:* people's feelings of control over resources, decisions, actions, events, and activities
- *Responsibility:* people's ability to be accountable for their own actions
- *Unity:* the solidarity of groups of which people are members
- *Place:* places where people feel at ease
- *Location:* locales to which people have historical, cultural, or social ties

These concepts echo features described by Guba and Lincoln (1989) in their book *Fourth Generation Evaluation.* Their hermeneutic dialectic process, or meaning-making dialogue, requires interactions that respect people's dignity, integrity, and privacy through the following:

- Full participatory involvement
- Political parity of those involved
- Consensual, informed, sophisticated joint construction
- Conceptual parity
- Refusal to treat individuals as subjects or objects of study

The implicit assumption in these ideas is that procedural matters that directly affect the quality of people's lives need to be taken into account, not only for humanitarian or ethical reasons but also for underlying pragmatic purposes. As Guba and Lincoln put it so succinctly, attention to these properties is likely to "unleash energy, stimulate creativity, instill pride, build commitment, prompt the taking of responsibility, and evoke a sense of investment and ownership" (p. 227).

The Role of the Researcher

The assumptions delineated above dramatically change the role of the person who is traditionally called "the researcher." In community-based action research, the role of the researcher is not that of an expert who *does* research but that of a resource person. He or she becomes a facilitator or consultant who acts as a catalyst to assist stakeholders in defining their problems clearly and to support them as they work toward effective solutions to the issues that concern them. Titles such as *facilitator, associate,* and *consultant* are more appropriate in community-based action research than *director, chief,* or *head,* which are common to more hierarchical operations. The language signals the nature of relationships and the orientation of the research. A group of community workers in Western Australia characterized their community-based work in this way (Kickett, McCauley, & Stringer, 1986):

- You are there as a *catalyst.*
- Your role is not to impose but to *stimulate people* to change. This is done by addressing issues that concern them *now.*
- The essence of the work is *process—the way things are done—*rather than the result achieved.
- The key is to *enable people to develop their own analysis* of their issues.
- Start where people are, not where someone else thinks they are or ought to be.
- Help people to analyze their situation, consider findings, plan how to keep what they want, and change what they do not like.
- Enable people to examine several courses of action and the probable results or consequences of each option. After a plan has been selected it is the worker's role to *assist in implementing* the plan by raising issues and possible weaknesses and by helping to locate resources.

- The worker is not an advocate for the group for which he or she works.
- The worker does not focus only on solutions to problems but on *human development.* The responsibility for a project's success lies with the people. (p. 5)

This "bottom-up" or grassroots orientation uses stakeholding groups as the primary focus of attention and source of decision making. It is an approach that requires research facilitators to work in close collaboration with stakeholders and to formulate "flat" organizational structures that put decision-making power in stakeholders' hands.

This approach differs from the authoritarian manner that is, unfortunately, all too common in institutional and organizational life. People in positions of power tend to assume that being organizationally superior, they have superior knowledge. We have all experienced or observed the authoritarian teacher, administrator, director, social worker, or expert who is feared and/or mistrusted by clients and organizational inferiors, the autocrat who demands that work be carried out according to his or her dictates. This type of tyranny represents the extreme end of a spectrum of authority but is, to a greater or lesser extent, embedded in the hierarchical operations of many institutions and organizations. Such authority is based on the premise that managers, administrators, policymakers, or "representatives," because of their knowledge of the big picture, are best able to make decisions for client groups and constituencies.

In many situations, this expectation runs contrary to the lived experience of the people. "Experts" are usually trained in narrow areas and often cannot understand the intricacies and complexities of people's lives. "Representatives" often speak for only one group in a constituency and reflect perspectives and interests of that group alone. Moreover, many of the procedures used to try to broaden inputs from constituent groups are so flawed as to be of little value. Surveys, for instance, are usually limited in scope and are frequently riddled with the agendas, interests, and perspectives of the people who commission or construct them. Further, consultation processes frequently occur under conditions that inhibit the participation of many constituent groups.

A colleague referred to community consultation techniques used by government agencies in his state as processes of "insultation." People usually were asked to attend meetings in places such as schools, public offices, libraries, or upscale hotels, venues that were either inaccessible to people who lacked private transport or socially or culturally alien to them. Meetings often were held at times or under conditions that prevented the attendance of women with children, employed people, poor people, and members of minority groups. The processes of consultation tended to be dominated by those who happened to have no work or home responsibilities or had the personal resources to make themselves available at times suited to the institution or the bureaucracy.

I have been present at many meetings at which "representatives" have provided the basis for significant changes to community life. In one instance, I attended a community consultation meeting with senior politicians and government bureaucrats who wished to gain input on government policy initiatives. It was held at a time when most people in that town were unavailable, so that two vocal young women with little standing in the community became the focus of the consultative process. The only other participants were retired people who were given little information about the nature of the processes in which they were involved and appeared to be puzzled by the discussions that took place.

The politicians and bureaucrats who flew into town about noon flew out less than 3 hours later, apparently happy with their "community consultation." I have little doubt that any action that resulted from that visit was not well received by people in the community. They almost certainly would have been insulted by the paucity of the consultation process and would have perceived any actions as the imposition of outside authority on their lives.

In many situations, individuals tend to react negatively to authoritarian processes. When the imposition of outside authority has an impact on their lives, even if with the best of intentions, they often respond with

Aggression, directed at those who are controlling their lives

Apathy, which sucks their vitality and leaves them with feelings of hopelessness or helplessness

Avoidance, which isolates them from the source of authoritarian control

When working with people, we as practitioners need to create the conditions that will mobilize their energy, engage their enthusiasm, and generate activity that can be productively applied to the resolution of issues and problems that concern them.

Working Principles

Community-based research seeks to develop and maintain social and personal interactions that are nonexploitative and enhance the social and emotional lives of all people who participate. It is organized and conducted in ways that are conducive to the formation of community—the "common unity" of all participants—and that strengthen the democratic, equitable, liberating, and life-enhancing qualities of social life. The principles delineated below—concerning relationships, communication, participation, and inclusion—can help practitioners in formulating activities that are sensitive to the key elements of this mode of research.

Relationships

Whenever I commence work with a new group of people, the words of my good friend Doug come constantly to mind. "Relationships are the key," he constantly reminds us. I have had many opportunities to witness the wisdom encompassed in that small phrase. There have been times when projects have come to a grinding halt, or disappeared almost without trace, because of antagonisms that developed between participants. Although I have experienced many situations in which I have been able to maintain productive working relationships with people whom, quite frankly, I did not like, I struggle to remember situations in which I have been able to work successfully with people toward whom I have had hostile feelings, or who have had hostile feelings toward me. As Doug says, relationships are the key!

The type, nature, and quality of relationships in any social setting will have direct impacts on the quality of people's experience and, through that, the quality of outcomes of any human enterprise. Community-based action research has a primary interest, therefore, in establishing and maintaining positive working relationships (see Box 2.2).

BOX 2.2
Relationships in Action Research

Relationships in action research should
- Promote feelings of equality for all people involved
- Maintain harmony
- Avoid conflicts, where possible
- Resolve conflicts that arise, openly and dialogically
- Accept people as they are, not as some people think they ought to be
- Encourage personal, cooperative relationships, rather than impersonal, competitive, conflictual, or authoritarian relationships
- Be sensitive to people's feelings

Key concepts: equality, harmony, acceptance, cooperation, sensitivity

---

Practitioners who have worked in organizational settings know the destructive impact on work life of relationships gone wrong. When antagonisms develop or persons in positions of authority act autocratically, the quality of work is likely to deteriorate, and workers are likely to find their emotional and physical well-being at risk. In such an environment, the conditions for productive and harmonious work do not exist.

A new manager was appointed to supervise the work of a group of social workers with whom I was acquainted. Having little experience in the work of these experienced practitioners, and being ambitious, she set out to impress her superiors with her efficiency and effectiveness. She embarked on projects that her staff considered inappropriate and put great pressure on them to work in ways that she perceived to be efficient. In the process, she tried to have them act in ways that were contrary to their previously effective work routines and constantly referred to her superior, the director, when they disputed her direction.

Within a short time, work conditions deteriorated dramatically. The social workers struggled to maintain their operation and, in the process, experienced great frustration and stress, to the extent that they started to experience both physical and emotional problems. One staff member took a series of extended leaves, another began visits to a psychiatrist, and another transferred to a different section, her position being filled by a series of temporary workers. Eventually, the manager, also under stress, left the agency, and the entire section was disbanded.

The situation I have just described is, unfortunately, not an isolated one. Practitioners who have worked in organizational or institutional settings for any length of time will find the scenario all too familiar.

Marxist theory suggests that relationships in capitalist societies are determined by the demands of economic production and are inherently oppressive. It suggests that those who control the means of production cast people into forms of relationship based on force and manipulation. These patterns of relationship, the theory suggests, lead to extreme institutionalization based on authoritarian forms of control that become oppressive and dehumanizing as they fail to acknowledge the fundamental human needs of those involved in work settings. Although such a deterministic analysis is too simplistic when applied to modern liberal democratic societies, it does have a ring of truth about it and alerts us to the dangers of alienation that often accompany technological production and bureaucratic organization.

The work of Foucault (1979) is likewise instructive. Foucault suggests that forms of oppressive relationship are not "cast in stone" at the institutional level (i.e., by those at the top of the social hierarchy) but are instituted by power-discourse relations throughout all levels of a system. These power-discourse relations—ways of ordering activity through rules, regulations, and directives—orchestrate the techniques and practices by which social control and domination are exercised.

The force of these perspectives is to sensitize us to the need to be consciously aware of the nature of relationships in our everyday professional lives. It suggests the need to reject styles of interactions that emphasize status and power and to move to more consensual modes of operation. It implies the need to develop cooperative approaches to work and harmonious relations between and among people and to reject the aggressive, impersonal, and manipulative relations characteristic of many bureaucratic systems.

The desire to develop more equitable and liberating social relations implies a need for flatter organizational structures that minimize the social distance and power differentials among people. It emphasizes collegial or matrix organizational structures, rather than those based on hierarchy, and leadership roles that facilitate and support people rather than direct and control them. It alludes to the need to redefine systems of organizational reward so that people have no need to "climb on the backs of others" to gain a sense of accomplishment but are rewarded for the quality of their differing contributions.

When we seek to organize any set of activities within an organizational or community setting, we need to examine the type, nature, and quality of relationships among clients, practitioners, administrators, and other stakeholders. At the base of a productive set of relationships is people's ability to feel that their ideas and agendas are acknowledged and that they can make worthwhile contributions to the common enterprise. This, ultimately, is at the core of a democratic society.

I am reminded of one of the really fine school principals with whom I served. He was, to me, a leader in the fullest sense of the word. Knowledgeable and skillful, he provided me, as a young teacher, with suggestions for ways to improve my teaching that did not imply that I was not already a capable teacher, suggesting or indicating the areas of weakness in my teaching without making me feel put down; he enhanced my feelings of competence and worth by praising my strengths. He was "Dick" to us teachers much of the time but became "Mr. Filmer" when the occasion warranted our serious attention, or in the more formal moments of ritualized school activities. The words gentleman and scholar in their best older senses come to my mind: He was a leader of stature and capability who still provides me with one of the touchstones by which I evaluate any leadership work in which I engage. Thank you, Dick Filmer.

Communication

When disparate groups of people are brought together to enact community-based action research, the nature and style of communication among people will have significant impacts on their ability to work together effectively. Communication has direct effects on feelings of well-being and can enhance or detract from the efficacy of individuals' work.

Community-based action research requires all participants to engage in styles and forms of communication that facilitate the development of harmonious relationships and the effective attainment of group or organizational objectives (see Box 2.3). German scholar Jürgen Habermas (1979) suggests that positive change originates from communicative action—the capacity for people to work through disagreements to achieve effective solutions to problems. His formulation of the "ideal speech situation" suggests four fundamental conditions that need to be met if communication is to be effective:

- *Understanding:* The receiver can understand what is being communicated.
- *Truth:* The information is accurate and is not a fabrication.
- *Sincerity:* The communicator is sincere in his or her attempts to communicate and has no hidden agendas.
- *Appropriateness:* The manner, style, and form of communication are appropriate to the people, the setting, and the activity.

Institutional and bureaucratic arenas, because of the nature of their organization and operation, provide many examples in which these conditions are not met. Understanding, for instance, is often inhibited by the use of jargon, complex language, or esoteric subject matter. Professional

---

BOX 2.3
Communication in Action Research

In effective communication, one
- Listens attentively to people
- Accepts and acts on what they say
- Can be understood by everyone
- Is truthful and sincere
- Acts in socially and culturally appropriate ways
- Regularly advises others about what is happening

Key concepts: attentiveness, acceptance, understanding, truth, sincerity, appropriateness, openness

---

workers sometimes use technical language that clients either cannot understand or cannot relate to their experience. Academics frequently speak in an idiom that mystifies practitioners and laypersons alike. In these instances, understanding is limited and communication is faulty.

People sometimes tell lies deliberately to misinform others. The issue of "truth" is much broader than this, however. Truth is brought to question when information is distorted or misrepresented in attempts to persuade or deceive. Inflated estimates of costs and unwarranted promises of the benefits of particular projects are but two ways in which practitioners can distort truth and damage communicative action. The slick salesperson and the expensive auto service are common images in our social life. They have their counterparts in institutional life, however, in the educator who promotes a particular pedagogical approach and the academic who inflates his or her research grants through basically deceptive promises.

Manipulation through the use of distorted information or failure to make covert agendas explicit is so common that it is often accepted as an unfortunate but necessary part of social, organizational, and political life. Damage to communicative action through untruthfulness, however, often leads to more general problems. When people have been tricked or duped, they are frequently unable to continue to work harmoniously with those they feel have cheated them, and the chances of productive and effective work taking place are diminished accordingly.

Sincerity also is at risk when social workers, counselors, teachers, health workers, and other practitioners are bored with their work and merely go through the motions of providing services to their clients. When their lack of sincerity is detected, communication is likely to break down. Practitioners are also likely to perceive the real agendas of administrators who engage in activities aimed at increasing their chances of promotion but that are not in the best interests of their workers or clients. Sincerity is an essential ingredient of communicative action.

In many situations, communication is jeopardized when people feel that the manner or style of the communication is inappropriate or that the person involved is not the appropriate person. When a person from the majority culture speaks for the interests of a minority group in the absence of an appropriate spokesperson, when an administrator makes decisions about a program or service without consulting his or her staff, and when academic experts with little field experience are responsible for professional training, effective communication is difficult to achieve.

I once argued with one of my female colleagues about the need for members of minority groups to speak for themselves in public forums and to be in control of their own affairs. I was unable to make my point clearly until I asked the question, "Would it be right for a man to be head of the National Organization for Women?" with the implication that a man could control the affairs of that organization, represent the interests of women, and present papers on women's needs at conferences. She saw the point immediately.

Apart from these basic conditions of communication, however, the manner, style, and organization of communicative activity will provide many cues and messages that can have significant impacts on people's feelings of well-being and their orientation to activities and agendas. When people feel acknowledged, accepted, and treated with respect, their feelings of worth are enhanced, and the possibility that they will contribute actively to the work of the group is maximized. Communication is the key to the effective operation of any process of inquiry.

Participation

To the extent that people can participate in the process of exploring the nature and context of the problems that concern them, they have the opportunity to develop immediate and deeply relevant understandings of their situation and to be involved actively in the process of dealing with those problems. The task in these circumstances is to provide a climate that gives people the sense that they are in control of their own lives and that supports them as they take systematic action to improve their circumstances (see Box 2.4).

BOX 2.4
Participation in Action Research

Participation is most effective when it
- Enables significant levels of active involvement
- Enables people to perform significant tasks
- Provides support for people as they learn to act for themselves
- Encourages plans and activities that people are able to accomplish themselves
- Deals personally with people rather than with their representatives or agents

Key concepts: involvement, performance, support, accomplishment, personalization

---

Until historically recent times, people were intimately involved in the production of goods and the delivery of services that were part of their day-to-day lives. The farms that surrounded villages provided employment as well as food and clothing, and storekeeper, smith, mason, and preacher were known to everyone who lived locally. Today, the large and centralized social systems that are characteristic of modern societies alienate people from those who provide for their well-being and from the decisions that affect their lives. People are increasingly subject to the faceless dictates of transnational corporations and state and federal agencies for their employment, health, education, and other aspects of community life.

Centralized control has the advantage of concentrating resources to foster large projects and programs—such as health and education systems—that have the capacity to improve or maintain the quality of life of large populations. The downside of centralized control is that those who determine the "texts" of these projects, programs, and services do so in ways that fit their own interests and agendas and the imperatives of their own social and cultural perspectives. A managerial and professional class dominates decision-making processes, often to the detriment of people from lower classes or cultural minorities. The decision makers determine how things will operate, who will benefit, under what circumstances, and according to which criteria.

In such situations, there is often a tendency to standardize procedures and practices according to managerial or professional cultural imperatives, on the assumption that these fit the general population, notwithstanding that any large population will vary greatly according to the social groups that constitute it. Social identities related to class, ethnicity, race, religion, age, gender, locality, employment, and leisure activities will relate to divergent lifestyles, beliefs, customs, mores, morals, values, skills, knowledge, understanding, and behavioral propensities. When the social and cultural perspectives of a group diverge significantly from those necessary for the group to take advantage of the standardized procedures developed by central policymakers, problems are likely to occur.

Control always has been a significant factor in bureaucratic life, and supervisory roles increasingly are framed in control-oriented managerial terms. Although there is nothing necessarily problematic about framing leadership activity as management, the language of that discipline tends to reflect the ethos of the corporate world in which it was nurtured. There is a tendency to incorporate the values and agendas of the corporate world, with its emphasis on profit, production, and control, into all areas of social, educational, and welfare life—to frame projects according to economic or technical agendas, for instance, while social, cultural, emotional, and spiritual issues fade into obscurity.

The post-World War II relocation of poor and working-class people from sprawling urban neighborhoods into high-rise housing projects is a clear example of the dominance of this perspective. The rich and integrated social networks and vital sense of community that existed in those older neighborhoods were destroyed to provide low-cost housing. Ugly and featureless high-rise ghettos now characterize life for many urban poor and working-class people in modern industrial nations. The results of such development in parts of Chicago, London, Los Angeles, and many other cities can be seen in the social statistics and media reports on crime, drug abuse, and violence that relate to these sites.

Many similarly misguided projects have had their genesis in perceptions that technical or managerial expertise can determine what is best for people. Practitioners are currently becoming more aware of the limitations of that expertise, however, and there is an increasing tendency to engage clients, patients, consumers, and students in decision-making processes. We have also become more sensitive to the view that an army of experts is unlikely to be able to meet people's needs if the people themselves remain merely passive recipients of services. As practitioners in many fields now realize, unless people come to understand procedures and practices by participating in their development, any program or service is likely to have limited effects on their lives. Patients who fail to maintain appropriate health practices, passive and disinterested students, recalcitrant welfare recipients, disorderly youth, and families in crisis will often not respond to the authoritative dictates of the "experts" whose task it is to solve their problems.

A colleague of mine once had the task of presenting training programs on alcohol and drug abuse. Most of the participants were enrolled under court order, as part of their sentences for drug and/or alcohol-related offenses. The program, which included information about the physical and psychological effects of alcohol and other drugs, was presented to an audience that was, from my colleague's accounts, almost completely unreceptive. "You could tell that they didn't want to be there, and that they wouldn't believe anything I said to them anyway," he commented. "It was a real waste."

I previously had been involved in a workshop given by a senior academic to a community group that had requested a program that would help them better understand the devastating effects of alcohol consumption. The workshop included exploration of a complex three-factor model of drinking behavior that taxed my intellectual capabilities and required considerable concentration on the part of the other participants. As the workshop progressed, they pointed out that the model was inadequate relative to some of the realities of their community life and suggested modifications that would improve it. All participants worked energetically throughout the afternoon, to the extent that the facilitator commented that he was able to cover more ground in that afternoon than he could in 3 weeks of course work with his postgraduate students. The energy, involvement, and motivation of the participants reflected their orientation to the processes of the workshop. It made sense from their perspective and spoke to issues that concerned them.

Community-based action research seeks to engage people directly in formulating solutions to problems they confront in their community and organizational lives. It is the researcher's task to facilitate and support these activities, rather than to determine their direction. Administration and management evolve from arrangements whereby the various stakeholder groups—practitioners, clients, administrators, and community members—participate in significant ways in planning and decision making. Leadership, in this instance, is defined according to its function of facilitating organizational and operational processes, rather than defining and controlling them. Active participation is the key to feelings of ownership that motivate people to invest their time and energy to help shape the nature and quality of their community lives.

Inclusion

Community-based action research seeks to enact an approach to inquiry that includes all relevant stakeholders in the process of investigation. It creates contexts that enable diverse groups to negotiate their various agendas in an atmosphere of mutual trust and acceptance and to work toward effective solutions to problems that concern them (see Box 2.5).

BOX 2.5
Inclusion in Action Research

Inclusion in action research involves
- Maximization of the involvement of all relevant individuals
- Inclusion of all groups affected
- Inclusion of all relevant issues—social, economic, cultural, political—rather than a focus on narrow administrative or political agendas
- Ensuring cooperation with other groups, agencies, and organizations
- Ensuring that all relevant groups benefit from activities

Key concepts: individuals, groups, issues, cooperation, benefit

---

A feature of modern life is the concentration of power in the hands of small groups of people. In public life, "representatives," "leaders," or "managers" are given decision-making power over large groups to enable them to control and organize activities. As a consequence, participation in the organizational lives of schools, health agencies, and other community institutions is often characterized by the dominance of middle-class professional groups and, particularly, administrative interests. Management is greatly affected by the needs to play off the agendas of the various client groups and to deal with political machinations that often arise. In these circumstances, the desire for smoothly administered programs limits the extent to which administrators are willing to tolerate the intimate involvement of their diverse and sometimes antagonistic clients. Administrators therefore often focus decision-making processes on an inner circle of their staff or maintain control through truncated decision-making procedures. Committee membership is often carefully controlled to ensure that only restricted groups of people are involved, and meeting agendas are regulated judiciously.

In these circumstances, the voices of the most powerless groups tend to go unheard, their agendas ignored and their needs unmet. Organizational procedures often operate according to administrative priorities and fail to accommodate the social and cultural imperatives that dominate people's lives. Problems proliferate as practitioners struggle to cope with escalating crises that result from the failure of programs and services to cater to client needs. Moreover, these pressures are sometimes exacerbated by political or community demands that "something be done." All too often, superficial solutions provide the semblance of immediate action but in effect can actually exacerbate the situation.

Lawmakers in the United States have recently enacted legislation that increases penalties for criminal offenses, responding to a growing chorus in the country to send young "criminals" to prison and to extend their sentences. In a country with the third-highest rate of incarceration in the world, the likely outcome of these pressures will be to increase, rather than decrease, criminal activity. I remember the words of a friend of mine who, in his earlier years, had "done time" for a number of offenses. His time in prison had, apart from anything else, increased his criminal skills considerably. He had learned a number of ways to break into and start cars, how to break into stores and houses, how to dispose of stolen goods, and how to evade capture. The major outcome of his prison experience was an increase in the extent of his criminal skills and knowledge.

The potential payoff for opening up the processes of organizational life is enormous. Not only does it provide the possibility of increased human resources, but it creates conditions likely to lead to the formation of operational processes that are socially and culturally appropriate for diverse client groups. By including people in decisions about the programs and services that serve them, practitioners extend their knowledge base considerably and mobilize the resources of the community. Including more people in the process may seem to increase the possibilities for complexity and conflict, but it also enables practitioners to broaden their focus from one that seeks the immediate resolution of specific problems to more encompassing perspectives that have the potential to alleviate many interconnected problems.

Note

1. Kelly and Sewell (1988) differentiate five approaches to community building: service delivery, advocacy (brokering), community action (campaigning), community development, and intentional community.

BOX 2.6
Working Principles of Community-Based Action Research

Relationships in action research should
- Promote feelings of equality for all people involved
- Maintain harmony
- Avoid conflicts, where possible
- Resolve conflicts that arise, openly and dialogically
- Accept people as they are, not as some people think they ought to be
- Encourage personal, cooperative relationships, rather than impersonal, competitive, conflictual, or authoritarian relationships
- Be sensitive to people's feelings

In effective communication, one
- Listens attentively to people
- Accepts and acts on what they say
- Can be understood by everyone
- Is truthful and sincere
- Acts in socially and culturally appropriate ways
- Regularly advises others about what is happening

Participation is most effective when it
- Enables significant levels of active involvement
- Enables people to perform significant tasks
- Provides support for people as they learn to act for themselves
- Encourages plans and activities that people are able to accomplish themselves
- Deals personally with people rather than with their representatives or agents

Inclusion in action research involves
- Maximizing the involvement of all relevant individuals
- Including all groups affected
- Including all relevant issues—social, economic, cultural, political—rather than a focus on narrow administrative or political agendas
- Ensuring cooperation with other groups, agencies, and organizations
- Ensuring that all relevant groups benefit from activities

3

Setting the Stage

The Basic Routine Revisited

The purposes of community-based action research are to enable systematic investigation and resolution of problems experienced by practitioners and their clients, to examine the effectiveness of their work practices, and to take methodical action to resolve those problems. Although practitioners will apply general processes of inquiry routinely to their everyday work and professional lives, deep-seated, persistent, or extensive problems may require a more rigorous and sustained process of investigation. In these circumstances, an individual or small group may take responsibility for facilitating or leading the process. In this and the chapters that follow, I approach research processes from the perspective of the research facilitator. Practitioners who engage in their own research may adapt their reading accordingly.

In Chapter 2, I introduced the three fundamental steps of a basic action research routine. In the first phase—*look*—participants *define and describe* the problem to be investigated and the general context within which it is set. In the second phase—*think*—they *analyze and interpret* the situation to extend their understanding of the nature and context of the problem. In the third phase of the process, they *act* to formulate *solutions* to the problem.

This simple routine, however, masks a complex array of influences and activities. Multiple viewpoints and agendas constantly disrupt proceedings, resulting in a continuous need to negotiate perspectives and modify and adapt actions. The research task becomes a social process in which people reconstruct their lives together through continuing cycles of exchange, negotiation, realignment, and repair. Research events, therefore, become more interactive and repetitive as multiple descriptions, analyses, and explanations are interwoven in a complex process of inquiry.

The first task of an action research process requires participants to become familiar with the complexity that surrounds them. Research facilitators, in particular, will need to construct systematically a picture of the situation in which they are working to locate the individuals and groups with whom they will work and to formulate a preliminary understanding of their situation. In the remainder of this chapter, I provide a reminder of the constructive, meaning-making processes in which we are engaged and then describe a set of procedures that enable research facilitators to set the stage for research activity. The preliminary activities include ways of establishing contact, establishing the researcher's role in the process, identifying stakeholding groups and key people within them, and constructing a preliminary picture of the research context.

Negotiation, Consensus, and Construction

The art and craft of community-based action research include the careful management of research activities so that stakeholders can formulate jointly constructed definitions of the situation. Egon Guba and Yvonna Lincoln (1989) suggest that

> the major task of the constructivist investigator is to tease out the constructions that various actors in a setting hold and, so far as possible, to bring them into conjunction—a joining—with one

another and with whatever other information can be brought to bear on the issues involved. (p. 142)

Constructions are created realities that exist as integrated, systematic, sense-making representations and are the stuff of which people's social lives are built. The aim of inquiry is *not* to establish the truth or to describe what really is happening but to reveal the different truths and realities—constructions—held by different individuals and groups. Even people who have the same facts or information will interpret them differently according to their experiences, worldviews, and cultural backgrounds. The task of the community-based action researcher, therefore, is to develop a context in which individuals and groups with divergent perceptions and interpretations can formulate a construction of their situation that makes sense to them all—a joint construction. Guba and Lincoln (1989) designate this a *hermeneutic dialectic process*, because new meanings emerge as divergent views are compared and contrasted. The major purpose of the process is to achieve a higher-level synthesis, to reach a consensus where possible, to otherwise expose and clarify the different perspectives, and to use these consensual/divergent views to build an agenda for negotiating actions to be taken. The hermeneutic dialectic process is fundamental to community-based action research, requiring people to work together with purpose and integrity to ensure the effective resolution of their issues and problems.

Because this activity brings people's work lives, and sometimes private lives, into the public arena, it requires a great deal of tact and sensitivity. Construction, consensus, and negotiation need to take place in conditions that recognize the impacts of these activities on participants' pride and dignity and that enhance their feelings of unity, control, and responsibility. The routines described below, therefore, reflect a commitment to the working principles discussed in the preceding chapter and summarized here in Box 3.1. At every stage of their work, research facilitators should ensure that procedures are in harmony with these guidelines, constantly checking that their actions promote and support people's ability to be active agents in the processes of inquiry. The underlying principle here is that human purposes are at least as important as technical considerations.

BOX 3.1
Principles of Community-Based
Action Research

Relationships that are
- Equal
- Harmonious
- Accepting
- Cooperative
- Sensitive

Communication that is
- Attentive
- Accepting
- Comprehensible
- Truthful
- Sincere
- Appropriate
- Advisory

Participation that is
- Involving
- Active
- Supportive
- Successful
- Personal

Inclusion that accounts for
- All individuals
- All groups
- All issues
- Cooperation
- Benefit

Looking at the Lay of the Land:
Preliminary Activity

The purpose of preliminary activity is to establish a positive climate of interaction and activity that engages the energy and enthusiasm of all stakeholders. Programs, projects, and services that fail to capture the interest or commitment of the people they serve are often ineffective, inefficient, or both. Practitioners often assume that they can implement a program once they have gained official permission, only to discover that client groups refuse to participate. I have spoken with practitioners in many fields who have been frustrated by their inability to engage people in activities that appear, from their own perspective, to be highly desirable. Their comments and questions tend to resemble the following:

- How can we get parents to participate in classroom activities? We can't even get them to come to the school.
- These young people must help us if we're to develop this facility for them.
- The mothers should bring their babies to the clinic more regularly, but they won't.
- We just can't seem to stop these kids from drinking or taking drugs or engaging in sex.

The language these practitioners use provides clues to the social dynamics involved. When we try to get people to do anything, insist that they must or should do something, or try to stop them from engaging in some activity, we are working from an authoritative position that is likely to generate resistance. Such situations often are characterized by processes in which people in positions of authority already have defined the problem and formulated a solution. They fail to grasp that others may interpret the situation and/or the significance of the problem in ways different from their own or may have different agendas in their lives, with other matters having much higher priority. My experience suggests that programs and projects begun on the basis of the decisions and definitions of authority figures have a high probability of failure.

I have seen many housing projects that failed miserably because of inadequate consultation with community members. In one community I visited regularly, the building coordinator was consistently frustrated in his attempts to hire local labor and failed to understand that the housing project had been imposed in that locality with little attempt to include members of the community in the planning phase. The building authority had met with two community leaders and had made determinations on that basis. Other sections of the community were, quite understandably, somewhat affronted by some aspects of the plan and failed to invest their energies. Problems multiplied in the community from that time on.

The processes described below are designed to furnish a context that will stimulate stakeholders' energies and inspire them to invest their time and personal resources. Preliminary activity also enables research facilitators to discover the makeup of the setting and establish a presence in that context.

▒ Establishing Contact

In the early stages of a research project, it is important for facilitators to establish contact with all stakeholder groups as quickly as possible. Each group needs to be informed of events and to feel that all members can contribute to the research processes. A stranger who is heard speaking to some groups about issues of concern to other groups may arouse suspicion, antagonism, and fear. With that in mind, research facilitators should place a high priority on identifying stakeholders and informing them of the purpose of their activities.

Initial contact should be informative and neutral. A statement such as the following would be appropriate:

> I'm Ernie Stringer. I've been employed by the Watertown Council to work with unemployed single parents. Some people seem to think there is a problem. I'm not sure if anything needs to be done, but I thought that I might talk with people to find out what they think.

This type of introduction provides a general context for a community-wide conversation. After contact has been established, a process of communication should be formulated, for example, "Thanks for talking with me. You've been most informative. I'd really like to talk with you again. Would that be possible?"

Facilitators should establish convenient times and places to meet with people and should, after initial visits, contact people regularly. This way, people are more likely to feel that they are included in the process, that their input is significant, and that the project is theirs in some fundamental sense. This condition of *ownership* is an important element of community-based action research.

When research facilitators talk with people, they should also ask about others who should be included in discussions. This will extend the facilitator's knowledge about the membership of each group and of the different stakeholder groups. Networking, in this context, is not merely a political tool to be used to gain advantage but a social tool that ensures that all stakeholders are included in the process.

Identifying Stakeholding Groups

Practitioners come into contact with many types of people in their work in social, community, and organizational settings. Teachers' work, for instance, is directly affected by colleagues, administrators, support staff, students, and parents, but teachers also come into occasional contact with government officials, police, social workers, community leaders, church leaders, and many others. Workers in the health professions likewise find themselves in contact with nurses, paraprofessionals, doctors, support staff, patients, and administrators. Social workers and agency staff are affected by the wide range of people who work in their agencies, provide services or support to their agencies, and are clients of their agencies. Problems experienced by any of these groups are likely to affect the lives or work of all who have a stake in the situation.

Researchers, therefore, need to ensure that all stakeholders—people whose lives are affected—participate in defining and exploring the problem or service under investigation. Although it is not possible for all people to be thus engaged, it is imperative that all stakeholder groups feel that someone is speaking for their interests and is in a position to inform them of what is going on.

Research facilitators should conduct a social analysis of the setting to ensure that all relevant groups are included in the research process. Such a social analysis should identify the groups that have a stake in the problem under consideration, so that men and women from all age, social class, ethnic, racial, and religious groups, in all agencies, institutions, and organizations, feel that they have a voice in the proceedings. It is important to cut across these categories to ensure adequate representation—a middle-class migrant person cannot always speak for lower-class migrant people, an older person for youth, or men for women. Members of groups that do not have voices in the proceedings will likely fail to invest themselves in the research processes and may then undermine any resulting activity.

In many settings, I see middle-class professional people making decisions about programs and services that serve the needs of people about whom they have little understanding. The failure of schools to provide for the learning needs of minority populations signals the failure of school systems to engage minority people in the processes of educational planning. In one Australian town that I know, issues related to Aboriginal students are usually referred to a local Aboriginal pastor, although he represents only one of the Aboriginal groups there. The pastor speaks from the perspective of a Christian Aboriginal person and sometimes neglects the interests of other groups who are more closely bound to their traditional spiritual heritage.

This is not an unusual situation. I have observed many instances in which certain people from a minority group are chosen to speak for all others because their middle-class social skills make them acceptable to mainstream institutions, despite their alienation from the people they are asked to represent.

Youth programs often are set up so that well-mannered, clean-living, decent young people are inducted into courses intended to provide them with leadership skills that will enable them to provide appropriate direction to their peers and thus prevent drug problems, teenage pregnancy, and so on. Participants rarely are chosen by their peers, and few are closely related to the groups of young people who are actively taking drugs or engaging in sex. The real leadership in these situations is ignored in favor of the types of youths preferred by adult community leaders.

I participated in a training workshop in which agency workers sought ways of working with the members of a community group to stop them from drinking so much alcohol. The question asked was, "What can *we* do to stop *them* from drinking? (my emphases). The answer, I thought at the time, was, "Precious little!"

Social mapping processes can help researchers identify all groups and subgroups affected by the issue at hand so that they can fashion a comprehensive picture of the stakeholders in the setting. Charting the social dimensions of a setting can be useful in enabling people to visualize the diversity of groups in any social setting. All groups may not be involved in the research process, but the charting of stakeholders will help research participants identify those people who are primarily concerned with the issues at hand—sometimes known as the *critical reference groups.* Table 3.1 is similar to such a chart constructed by researchers who wished to identify the different groups in a Texas school district. Another version of the same table identified gender groups, so that each row was split into male and female. For other purposes, it may be necessary to define categories for age groups. The information may be recorded in tabular or descriptive form, although a map of the context that locates groups physically is sometimes illuminating.

TABLE 3.1 Stakeholder Groups

	Anglo			*African American*			*Hispanic*			*Asian*		
	Poor	*Middle-Class*	*Well-Off*	*Poor*	*Middle-Class*	*Well-Off*	*Poor*	*Middle-Class*	*Well-Off*	*Poor*	*Middle-Class*	*Well-Off*
Students												
Families												
Teachers												
Administrators												
Businesses												
Churches												
Service agencies												

▓ Identifying Key People

Researchers sometimes feel disconcerted when people fail to engage in projects that the researchers consider to be significant. They are often surprised when obstacles appear without warning, when people fail to attend meetings, when tasks are not performed, or when antagonism is directed toward them. In many such instances, they have not only transgressed the boundaries of people's symbolic territory but failed to obtain permission to enter that territory.

An important preliminary task for research facilitators is to determine the formal structure of relevant organizations. They need to identify and communicate with people in positions of influence and authority and gain their permission to work there, when that is organizationally appropriate. They also need, at the same time, to locate informal patterns of influence to ensure that all significant people— sometimes called *opinion leaders* or *gatekeepers*—are included in the early stages of the research process.

In one community project I observed, the agency worker took pains to identify all key people. After 2 months, he became aware that many of the activities he was promoting were failing to make headway, despite positive responses from many of the townspeople. He eventually discovered that one of the farmers in the district who came to town infrequently was a key person in a number of groups in town. He was highly respected and had a significant impact on community affairs. Once the worker contacted this farmer and talked through the issues with him, many of the obstacles simply disappeared.

▓ Establishing a Role

Traditionally, researchers have carried with them the aura and status of the expert/scientist, expecting and being accorded deference. In action research, however, the role and function of the researcher differ considerably from that model. No longer laden with the onerous task of discovering generalizable truths, the researcher takes on a role that carries with it a unique status that, in a very real sense, must be established in the context of each study.

The facilitator, therefore, first must establish a stance that is perceived as legitimate and nonthreatening by all major stakeholding groups. Problems will soon emerge if the researcher is perceived as a stranger prying into people's affairs for little apparent reason or as an authority attempting to impose an agenda. Although the researcher usually will be there under the auspices of some authority, that fact alone is insufficient to engage the attention or the cooperation of all groups in the setting. In many situations, associations with authority may be a marked hindrance, especially if people perceive that the researcher is there to judge, control, or interfere in their affairs.

Researchers, therefore, need to negotiate their role not only with those in positions of authority but with all the relevant stakeholder groups in the setting. The development of the role of the research facilitator in these circumstances can be conceptualized as having three elements: agenda, stance, and position.

Agenda

Research facilitators can establish their presence in a setting by informing people of their purpose. Initial introductions should include information, in a nondefinitive form, that invites questions and states the agenda in the broadest terms. Initial statements should provide the tacit understanding that the researcher is a resource person whose role is to assist stakeholders, rather than to prescribe their actions. Researcher roles and functions, therefore, become overtly articulated in the process of introduction. The people involved can begin to understand what the researcher is concerned with and the part he or she plays.

As inquiry proceeds, agendas will begin to emerge and become more clearly formulated. At this early stage, however, it is necessary only to establish the focus of activity in the most general terms.

Stance

A researcher's presentation of self should be as neutral and nonthreatening as possible. Body language, speech, dress, and behavior should be purposeful, inquiring, and unpretentious. The all-knowing stance of the expert, the authoritative demeanor of the boss, or the swagger of the achiever is likely to be detrimental to participatory investigation. Many people, especially those in subordinate positions, are likely to respond negatively to any such stance. Researchers should aim to present themselves in ways likely to be perceived as skilled, supportive, resourceful, and approachable. This does not mean that a passive demeanor is required. A friendly, purposeful stance is appropriate for most situations, although a more forceful approach may be appropriate when the researcher is dealing with prestigious or powerful people.

Position

Position can be thought of as three entities to which any group in a social setting may stake a claim: physical space, social status, and symbolic territory. A family clinic, although ostensibly available to the whole community, for instance, may be claimed by an informal group known as young mothers. A community center may be "owned" by a particular ethnic group. Part of a school ground may be recognized as belonging to a particular clique of girls. These examples show how informal groups, despite no formal legitimacy, have powerful impacts on social life. When researchers conduct their social analyses, it is imperative that they get to know the interacting networks of social groups and identities that cut across the boundaries of the formal organization of a community, institution, or agency. The physical and symbolic territory that such groups occupy will have significant impacts on the processes of investigation.

Networks of social identities are established more formally in such organizations as schools, hospitals, government agencies, social clubs, businesses, and churches. These institutions carefully delineate activities and allocate the people responsible for each territory. A high school English department, for instance, will operate under the leadership of a senior teacher who is accorded higher status than the other English teachers. The department will have responsibility for teaching English and related subjects and may be located in a particular part of the school building. A hospital trauma clinic will engage in medical emergency work, with orderlies, nurses, and doctors having different tasks and statuses—levels of importance—in that context. Churches will likewise allocate a variety of functions, statuses, and locations for worship, child and youth services, finances, and so on, to different groups or individuals.

Difficulties often arise when newcomers or people aspiring to change the status quo attempt to invade or change territory that is already occupied. The following comments illustrate situations in which people perceive that territorial boundaries have been crossed inappropriately:

- But Mrs. Jones and Miss Smith always have done the flowers.
- I'm a history teacher. How on earth can I teach English literature?
- Don Jones is part of my caseload. You have no right to interfere with him.
- Staff have never had access to the overall budget.
- The research methods class has never included qualitative methods before.

As researchers commence preparatory work, they should artfully position themselves so that they do not threaten the social space of the people with whom they will be working. They should take a neutral position with regard to their status, activities, and physical location, expressing interest but showing no signs that they have designs on any territory.

Research facilitators also cannot afford to be associated too closely with any one of the stakeholding groups in the setting. Members of all groups need to feel that they can talk freely with facilitators, without fear that their comments will be divulged to members of other groups whom, for one reason or another, they do not trust. They also need assurance that their perceptions and agendas will be considered consequential. Researchers, therefore, should endeavor to spend significant periods in places associated with each of the major stakeholder groups—the practitioner's workplace, the administrator's office, and the places where client services are provided. They should make themselves available constantly in these diverse settings so that all stakeholder groups feel that they have equal access. Visibility is important.

Researchers also should meet with people informally—in coffee shops, lunchrooms, sports arenas, bars, community centers, and even private homes, if invited. As they become known and accepted, they may tentatively request permission to attend events, meetings, activities, and so forth (e.g., "Would it be okay if I came along?"). The more freely researchers are able to participate in the ordinary lives of the people with whom they work, the more likely they are to gain the acceptance crucial to the success of community-based action research. By meeting with people in places where those people feel at home, researchers enable them to speak more freely and, in the process, acknowledge the significance of their cultural settings.

I have seen many mistakes made in all these areas—agenda, stance, and position—by otherwise well-intentioned researchers whose presentation of self effectively distanced or alienated them from those with whom they intended to work. I have seen social workers whose fashionable, high-quality clothing was in stark contrast to the cheap and worn clothing of their clients, serving as a constant reminder of the difference in their status. I have observed stylishly coiffed, manicured, and made-up teachers who were unaware of the subtle yet powerful messages their images presented to parents whose incomes and lifestyles were unable to sustain this type of presentation of self on a day-to-day basis. I have encountered researchers and agency workers who always visited the administrator first, disappearing into an office for extended conversations that raised the suspicions of workers and clients. In one instance, I spoke with a school psychologist who drove to her work in the poorest part of the city in an expensive Mercedes-Benz sports coupe. And in the case of the visiting politicians and bureaucrats mentioned in an earlier chapter, their suits and ties were in embarrassing contrast to the stained and worn clothing of their audience.

The agenda, stance, and positioning of research facilitators thus can have considerable impact on the success, or lack of success, of any community-based action research process. These elements of researchers' presentation carry many implicit messages that affect the extent to which other participants feel at home in the research process and are able to develop feelings of ownership. In summary, facilitators should take care to do the following:

- Present themselves as resource persons.
- Be aware of their dress and appearance.
- Establish their purpose in nonthreatening terms.
- Associate with all groups, formal and informal.
- Be visible.
- Be accessible.
- Meet in places where each of the stakeholder groups feels at home.

Constructing a Preliminary Picture

Initially, research facilitators should develop an understanding of the setting's social dynamics. They need to identify stakeholding groups, key people, the nature of the community, the purposes and organizational structure of relevant institutions and agencies, and the quality of relationships between and among individuals and groups.

Part of this process involves learning the history of the situation with which the researchers are concerned. This will be done in more detail at a later stage of the process, but researchers will need to know what has gone on with regard to key issues prior to their arrival. Past events sometimes leave legacies of deep hurts and antagonisms that severely limit prospects for successful projects unless they are handled judiciously.

A community agency in a country town contracted with the community services unit for which I worked to help with a problem that threatened to close down the agency's operations. The agency had been set up to provide developmental services to a number of community groups in the town and surrounding region. The government had discontinued funding, however, because it was alleged that the agency was no longer providing the services for which the funds had been provided. This was potentially a serious blow to a small community with limited resources.

We asked the agency executive committee and staff to provide their perspectives on the nature of the problem that had led to the current state of affairs. They provided a general picture of events (which was clarified further as different people presented their own parts of the story) that included the various groups and individuals who had been involved and the parts they had played. Participants in this process included the agency staff—development officer, bookkeeper, secretary, and field officer—and members of the executive committee—chair, secretary, and committee members. They also identified key people in the funding body—the regional manager and the field officers—as well as other individuals and groups who supported or were associated with the agency—members of a church group, the town clerk, and workers in a community agency in a nearby town.

We were given permission to contact each of these groups or individuals and proceeded to meet with them. I spoke first with the field officer of the funding body, and then the regional manager, taking care to maintain a friendly, nonthreatening, yet businesslike relationship and to have each of them describe the situation from his or her perspective. From their points of view, the agency had ceased to function effectively and staff members had become increasingly hostile each time they were approached to account for funds they had expended. I soon established that relations between the staff of the agency and the funding body were extremely antagonistic, making any communication problematic.

Reestablishing a working relationship between agency staff and officers of the funding body was difficult because agency staff members' attitudes seemed to change constantly. Although we discussed the need to establish a working relationship with the funding body and were able to arrange meetings with relevant people, agency workers would then quickly take a negative stance, criticizing the funding agency and decrying the activities of its workers. We eventually discovered that agency workers were meeting regularly with the agency's former bookkeeper, who fired them up each time they met about the deficiencies and character of the funding body officers.

We met with the former bookkeeper and talked through the issues with him, learning more about the history of the situation in the process and asking him to suggest what could be done. By incorporating his suggestions in our preliminary plan and asking his assistance to carry them out, we were able to defuse an uncomfortable situation that was hindering the project's progress.

The questions in the following list were used by one community worker to guide the building of his own preliminary picture of a particular situation (McCauley, 1985). It was a picture he kept for his own information only, and it differed from the pictures built by the community groups he worked with, but it served to orient him to the setting and to enable him to keep the "big picture" in mind. He was careful not to impose his picture on others or use it as a tool to define the reality of their situation:

- Relationships
    Who is related?
    How are they related?
- History
    When was the community started?
    Who were the founders?
    Why was it started?
    What has been the main economic base?
    Are the original families still there?
    What about the history of minority groups?
- Who's involved
    Important people
    Elected people
    Church people
    Government departments
    Local government
    Community leaders
    Community workers
- Groups
    Geographic groups
    Social groups
    Family groups

      Community groups

      Racial groups

      Ethnic groups

      Who is involved in each?

      Who are the key people?

      Which are the influential groups?

- Problems

      What problems do you see?

      What problems do others see?

      What problems do the power brokers see?

      What problems do local, state, and federal government offi-
         cers see?

      What problems do small groups see?

- Resources

      What social resources are available?

      What economic resources are available?

      Who owns them?

      Are they owned by individuals, groups, or government?

      What is missing?

      Why are they missing?

Research facilitators need to formulate their own questions according to the nature and extent of the inquiry in which they will engage. A more limited context, such as a classroom or agency office, may require a less extensive list of questions. The purpose of such questions is to ensure that researchers gain an adequate understanding of the setting in which they will work.

Sociable Research Processes

When we engage in research, we are not merely employing impersonal, technical routines that do not touch people's lives. The nature of any process of inquiry means that we enter cultural settings that are interactional, emotional, historical, and social. People interact at different times and places for different purposes, bringing histories of experience and understanding that orient them to the setting in particular ways.

They suffer stress, enjoy a joke, argue, play, work, and socialize in myriad ways that contribute to the life of the community.

The processes of community-based action research, therefore, are enriched by researchers who contribute to the lives of the groups with whom they work. Researchers increase their effectiveness when they immerse themselves in the richness of group life, talking with people about general events and activities, sharing a birthday cake, participating in informal or leisure activities, telling jokes, and so on. Scientific objectivity is not the purpose here. Although it is important to maintain a neutral stance in relation to micropolitical issues, participation entails the need to develop empathic understandings that come about only through close involvement with people. In these circumstances, community-based action research easily becomes an enjoyable human experience.

I've heard such comments as "All he does is sit around drinking coffee or tea with people"—remarks that especially in the early stages of a project, contain a grain of truth. I am constantly aware of the symbolic significance of sharing food and drink, so I always take people up on the offer of a cup of tea or coffee, a beer at a bar after work, dinner, a party, or a sporting event. I've been invited to church and into people's homes; I've sat in gardens drinking wine, watched basketball games, and attended school functions.

It's not only that I enjoy socializing—the activity is all part of my work, but it allows me to enter people's lives in a "real" way. These social activities break down barriers to communication, help me develop good working relations with others, and give me greater exposure to the setting in a relatively short time. It's surprising how much work can be done in these contexts. People in the course of social talk will often discuss issues related to the project. They become less guarded in such nonthreatening contexts and reveal much that in more formal contexts, they might have thought unimportant.

When this happens, I always make a formal visit to the people concerned soon afterward to ensure that they are comfortable with the conversation. I will say, "I had a great time with your friends yesterday. I enjoyed their company." Then, in the course of conversation, I also mention, "I was interested in what you had to say about . . . I didn't know that." This enables the other person to check that the confidentiality and safety of our conversations still hold in these contexts. The information is confirmed and often extended, and working relationships are strengthened in the process.

Conclusion

When we enact community-based action research processes, we are likely to engage approaches to work and community life that are at odds with the general conventions of the institutions and agencies that form the settings for much of our activity. The open dialogue that constitutes a core ingredient of our research processes runs the risk of disturbing a carefully controlled and regulated social environment. We probably will disturb micropolitical alignments and threaten people who have established positions of power and/or influence. In these circumstances, therefore, it is essential to ensure that our initial entry to the setting is as "soft" as possible. We need to understand the complex interactions among people, events, and activities and to comprehend the various ways in which they interpret their situations so that any activity we initiate sits easily in the minds of the people with whom we work.

Our ultimate goal is to provide a context that enables diverse stakeholders to work collaboratively toward solutions to the significant problems that confront them. The preliminary processes described in this chapter set the stage for this activity. They enable research facilitators to gain an overall picture of the situation, to develop positive relationships with people, and to help them think more deeply about their issues and concerns. The relationships and forms of communication that evolve set the stage for the inclusive and participatory processes that are the basis for common unity and productive action.

BOX 3.2
Looking at the Lay of the Land

PURPOSE:

Researchers/facilitators familiarize themselves with the research context

PROCESS:

Establish contact

Introduce yourself
Inform people of your interest

Identify stakeholding groups

Identify groups affected by the issue/agenda

Identify key people

Identify people in leadership positions and opinion leaders
Communicate with key people

Negotiate the researcher's role

Establish researcher's role: facilitator, leader, worker, etc.
Establish position of researcher: within which groups, in which places, doing what activities, with whom
Negotiate research agenda(s): which issue(s) will be the focus of inquiry

Build a preliminary picture of the context

Stakeholding groups
Key people
Institutions and agencies
The history of the issue

Look

BUILDING THE PICTURE

Constructing a New Vision

The objective of this stage of the process is for the researcher to assist stakeholders in describing their situation clearly and comprehensively. The activities presented in this chapter are designed for use by the researcher to assist stakeholders in *defining* the problem in their own terms and *describing* their work or community context in detail.

This exploration reveals the taken-for-granted visions and versions of reality that make up people's day-to-day life-worlds, bringing their unquestioned assumptions, views, and beliefs out in the open and displaying them for inspection. As people struggle to realize a collective vision/version of their world, they will discover perspectives that reveal new possibilities for resolving their problems. These collective visions may involve minor adjustments to people's own perspectives or may result in transformations that dramatically alter their worldviews. At best, this activity is liberating, enabling people to master their world as they see it in a different way—a tangible process of enlightenment.

At a community health workshop I attended, participants were asked to describe the types of drinking behavior displayed by various groups in their community. At the end of the workshop, one of the health workers exclaimed excitedly, "I used to see alcohol as a blanket covering my community. Now I see it in a different way. I can see the different ways that people use alcohol and the different outcomes of that use. Now I can see areas where things can be done." An explanatory framework that focused on descriptions of alcohol use, rather than alcoholism as a whole, resulted in a new vision that provided new possibilities for action.

This anecdote contains an important message: Problems do not exist in isolation but are part of a complex network of events, activities, perceptions, beliefs, values, routines, and rules—a cultural system maintained through the life of the group, organization, or community. As people reveal relevant details of their situation, they see more clearly the ways in which the research problem or focus is linked to features of their organizational, professional, and/or community lives. This disclosure leads people past their taken-for-granted perspectives and promotes more satisfying, sophisticated, and complete descriptions of their situation.

I worked with a group of high school students and their parents regarding a situation that had arisen at the local high school. The principal was attempting to institute (illegally, as it happened) a dress code in the school, and this had upset a significant number of students and parents. When I asked, "What is the problem here?" one of the students responded, "Jones [the principal] is a [expletive]," a comment greeted with a chorus of approval and similarly disapproving comments by other students.

Rather than continue to focus on the character of the principal, I asked the students, "What does he do?" This resulted in detailed information about the principal's actions. Through the use of neutral, but probing, questions, we compiled a much more complete picture of what was happening in the school, which proved to be of great interest to students and parents alike. In time, we were able to understand how the principal's vision of the school was enacted. This description included information not only about the dress code but also about many other features of the life of the school. As we extended our insight, it was apparent that the principal was instituting a conservative and authoritarian approach to education that ran contrary to the philosophy of many of the families in this progressive community.

Formulating a report that is a consensual account can be a demanding exercise. Organizational dictates often interact with personal and political agendas, interests, and needs to create the potential for division and conflict. Community-based action research, however, seeks a negotiated account that includes the perspectives, interests, and agendas of all parties. Described in the management literature as a "win, win, win" scenario, consensus is attained through careful processes of translation, modification, and accommodation.

Building the Picture

The task of research facilitators is to enable stakeholding groups to formulate jointly constructed descriptive accounts of the situation at hand. Each stakeholding group separately reports on its activities, then works with other groups to draft a joint report that provides a collaborative account of what they have achieved together. In the following sections, I describe how researchers facilitate this process by taking the following steps:

- Gathering information by
  Interviewing participants in each stakeholder group
  Participating in their work and/or community settings to observe activities and events
  Reading appropriate documents and records
- Constructing reports

Gathering Information

In Chapter 3, I described the preliminary activities through which research facilitators may gain a general understanding of the contexts in which they are working. As they meet with members of stakeholding groups, they systematically gather, record, and prepare information for use by stakeholders.

▒▒▒ Interviews

Interviews enable participants to describe their situation. The interview process not only provides a record of their views and perspectives but also symbolically recognizes the legitimacy of their views. An interview may occur naturally and comfortably during normal social interaction or may be undertaken more formally. In either case, researchers should do the following:

- Identify themselves, their role, and their purposes
- Ask permission to talk with people and to record information
- Check that the time is convenient for an extended discussion
- Negotiate alternative times and places for interviews, if necessary

As interviews progress, research facilitators may be presented with viewpoints that appear limited, biased, or wrong. They should, however, avoid discussion or debate with interviewees. Challenges to participant views will occur naturally as differing perspectives are presented in more public arenas. The task at this stage, to adapt the words of a well-known anthropologist, is "to grasp the natives' point of view, to realize their vision of their world" (Malinowski, 1922/1961, p. 25).

Questions

A major problem with the interview process is that questions are easily flavored by the researcher's perceptions, perspectives, interests, and agendas. Spradley (1979) provides a useful framework of relatively neutral and nonleading questions that minimize the extent to which participants' perceptions will be governed by frameworks of meaning inadvertently imposed by researchers. This framework is described below.

Grand tour questions are sufficiently global to enable participants to describe the situation in their own terms. They take the form, "Tell me about [your work]," which provides focus without giving direction or suggesting types or forms of responses. Other types of global question include the following:

- *Typical* questions, which enable respondents to talk of the ways events usually occur (e.g., "How does your group usually work?" "Describe a typical day in your office.")
- *Specific* questions, which focus on specific events or phenomena (e.g., "Can you tell me about yesterday's meeting?" "Describe what happened the last time . . . ")

Researchers can further extend accounts by using activities that enable participants to visualize their situation more clearly:

- A *guided tour* question is a request for an actual tour that allows participants to show researchers (and, where possible, other stakeholders) around their offices, schools, classrooms, clinics, centers, or agencies (e.g., "Could you show me around your center [office/classroom/clinic]?") Throughout the tour, participants may explain details about the people and activities involved in each part of the setting. Researchers may ask questions as they go (e.g., "Tell me more about this part of the clinic [room/office/class]." "Can you tell me more about the social workers [clients/patients/young people] you've mentioned?").
- A *task* question aids in description (e.g., "Could you draw me a map of the place you've described?"). Maps are often instructive and provide opportunities for extensive questioning and description. Participants can also demonstrate particular features of their work or community lives (e.g., "Can you show or tell me how you put a case study together?").

Further information may be acquired through the skillful use of *prompts* that enable participants to reveal more details of the phenomena they are discussing:

- *Extension* questions (e.g., "Tell me more about . . . " "Is there anything else you can tell me about?" "What else?")
- *Encouragement* comments or questions (e.g., "Go on." "Yes?" "Uh huh?")
- *Example* questions (e.g., "Can you give me an example of that?")

Once researchers have established a core of information through grand tour questions, they may gain more detailed information by pursuing a "minitour" that focuses on concepts already described (e.g., "You previously mentioned . . . Tell me more about that." "Can you describe a typical . . . ?"). Combinations of typical, specific, tour, task, extension, encouragement, and example questions provide opportunities for extensive exploration of the setting.

Research facilitators should take a neutral stance throughout these activities and neither affirm nor dispute, verbally or nonverbally, the information that emerges. At the same time, they should remain keenly attentive, recording responses as accurately as possible. It is essential that they capture participants' own terms and concepts for later use in formulating accounts.

Questions should be carefully formulated to ensure that participants are given maximum opportunity to present events and phenomena in their own terms and to follow agendas of their own choosing. Researchers should be particularly wary of leading questions that derive from their own interpretive schemata and are not directly related to participant agendas.

Tape Recorders

The use of a tape recorder has the advantage of allowing the researcher to record accounts that are both detailed and accurate. When used, tapes should be transcribed as soon as possible after the interview, and the researcher should verify the accuracy of the resulting text with the interviewee.

The use of tape recorders can have a number of disadvantages, however, and researchers should carefully weigh the merits of this technology. Technical difficulties with equipment may damage rapport with respondents, and people sometimes find it difficult to talk freely in the presence of a recording device, especially when sensitive issues are discussed. A researcher may need to wait until a reasonable degree of rapport has been established before introducing the possibility of using a tape recorder. When using a recorder, the researcher should be prepared to stop the tape to allow respondents to speak "off the record" if they show signs of discomfort.

▤ Participant Observation

As researchers meet members of stakeholding groups, they will have opportunities to gain a clearer picture of the research context by observing the settings in which participants live and work. They should record their observations in field notes that provide records of important elements of each part of the setting. Researchers should record these notes, which may include descriptions of the following types of elements, as soon after events as possible:

- *Places:* offices, homes, and community contexts; locations of activities and events; physical layouts
- *People:* individuals, types of people, formal positions, and roles
- *Objects:* buildings, furniture, equipment, and materials
- *Acts:* single actions that people take (e.g., reading a report on a client)
- *Activities:* a set of related acts (e.g., formulating a case study)
- *Events:* a set of related activities (e.g., case conference)
- *Purposes:* what people are trying to accomplish
- *Time:* times, frequency, duration, and sequencing of events and activities
- *Feelings:* emotional orientations and responses to people, events, activities, and so on

Observations enable researchers to record important details that become the basis for formulating descriptions from which stakeholding groups produce their accounts. Although field notes are commonly used for observations, videotapes and photographs may also provide a powerful record of events and activities.

As I talked with people in a community resource agency about their work, I also observed the conditions under which they worked, the resources available to them, the interactions among the different types of workers, and the tasks in which they were engaged. Through time, I gained a much clearer understanding of the operation of the agency than I had initially. I interviewed people and made similar observations during my visits to the funding agency with which the resource agency was in conflict and during visits to other relevant agencies and organizations in town. I recorded information about all these settings, noting those features that seemed relevant to the investigation. I returned to some of the settings to record more details as the need for more information arose. When agency workers complained of lack of equipment, materials, and stationery, for instance, I was able to assist them in performing a rough inventory and, in the process, was able to build a detailed picture of available resources.

I also visited key people in client groups and other agencies to acquire descriptive information about the general context of the town, the conditions in which its client groups lived, and other details of the community context. This information provided the materials from which I produced a general account of the context, which I presented as a preliminary report to the next meeting of the agency committee. I was careful to present an account that represented the situation as it was given to me by participants in the setting, including their differing perceptions and interpretations. I asked the committee to discuss each section of the report and then made modifications and additions on the basis of their comments.

Participation in research contexts also provides research facilitators with opportunities to engage in interviews and conversations that extend the pool of information available. Appropriate questions enable researchers to describe the situation in the participants' own terms. For instance,

- What are all the (places, acts, events, and the like)?
- Can you describe in detail the (objects, times, goals, and the like)?
- Can you tell me about all the (people, activities, and the like)? (Spradley, 1979, p. 79)

This process also provides opportunities for researchers to check the veracity of their own observations. Phenomena such as purpose and feeling can be inferred only superficially by an observer and need to be checked for accuracy. I might record, for instance, "The principal met faculty to present a written statement of the new school policy. The faculty appeared rather disgruntled with the new policy but made no comment about it." Here I have noted information related to (a) the purpose of the meeting and (b) the feelings of the faculty. This is potentially relevant information, but I would need to check with the principal and faculty to verify the authenticity of my interpretation. The principal may have other unstated purposes, the presentation of policy merely providing the context for meeting with faculty, and the faculty themselves may have been disgruntled about those other (hidden) agendas.

▨ Documents

Researchers can obtain a great deal of significant information by reviewing documents in the research context. They should search out relevant documents, ask about them during interviews, and request copies of the documents they observe in use. Documents may include memos, minutes, records, official reports, policy statements, procedure statements, plans, evaluation reports, press accounts, public relations materials, information statements, and newsletters.

Policy documents provide information about the nature of the organization or agency; annual reports and auditors' reports contain details of the structure, purposes, operations, and resources of the organization; and information statements and newsletters provide additional data sources. Confidential client records are not usually available for public scrutiny, and researchers need special circumstances and appropriate formal approval to gain access to them.

In some organizational environments, documentation is prolific. Researchers need to be selective, briefly scanning a range of documents to ascertain the information contained and its relevance to the project's focus. They should inspect official directories, where available, and keep records of the documents reviewed. They should record any significant information found in documents and note its source. In some cases, researchers may be able to obtain photocopies of relevant documents.

Researchers should prepare summary statements of information they have acquired and check them for accuracy with relevant stakeholders. In the process, they should ascertain which information may be made public and which must be kept confidential. The intent of the summaries is to provide stakeholders with information that enables each group (a) to review and reflect on its own activities and (b) to share relevant information with other stakeholding groups. This information will provide the key elements from which a jointly constructed account will be formulated.

Describing the Context:
Developing Descriptive Accounts

At this stage of the research process, participants should focus on developing detailed descriptions of the context within which events related to the issue investigated take place. This descriptive process should be done systematically to enable people to extend their understanding of the context and to clarify many aspects of the issue.

Described below are four alternative sets of procedures researchers may use to assist groups in formulating descriptive accounts of their situations. These are similar to processes used in ethnography and other forms of qualitative research and have been applied successfully in many community, organizational, and group contexts. Although each process is intended to provide a separate alternative approach to the development of a descriptive account, researchers may find, in practice, that they include any combination of the elements.

▨ Alternative 1: Working Ethnographically: Collaborative Descriptive Accounts

The processes outlined in the section on interviewing in this chapter may be applied to group contexts. Grand tour and other questions may be directed to a single group or to varied groups attending a meeting, instead of to individuals. The research facilitator should elicit multiple responses to these questions verbally, using group processes where appropriate, and record them in summary form on charts. This material can then be used in the formulation of descriptive accounts (see the section on formulating accounts below).

▨ Alternative 2: Six Questions: Why, What, How, Who, Where, When

The first question—why—provides a general orientation to the focus of the investigation, whereas succeeding questions—what, how, who, where, and when—enable participants to identify associated influences. The intent is not to define causes but to understand how the problem is encompassed in the context or setting. *How* and *what* questions are more productive than *why* questions. The former provide opportunities for revealing direct experience, whereas the latter often lead to causal explanations or forms of explanation that are remote from people's experience. Examples of appropriate initiating questions include the following:

- Why are we meeting today? What is the purpose?
- What is/are the problem(s)? What is happening?
- How does it affect our work/lives?
- Who is being affected?
- Where are things happening?
- When are things happening?

Answers should focus on acts, activities, and events related to the problem; participants should not attempt to evaluate or judge individual or group behavior. An initial pass through these questions will lead to further questions that can provide increasingly detailed information. This will include the history of the situation (how it came to be as it is), the people involved in or affected by the problem, interactions and relationships among these people, resources (people, space, time, funds—current use, access, availability), dreams, and aspirations.

▨ Alternative 3: Temporal Mapping: The Sequence of Events

Sociologist Norman Denzin (1989) suggests a similar procedure, which he terms *temporal mapping*—an account based on a sequence of events. Participants record descriptions of the problem and its context, and then "bracket" the information. That is, they take their descriptions apart, dissecting them to uncover key elements or essential features of the issue investigated. These elements are integrated into a descriptive account detailing the sequence of events and other relevant features of the context. The process requires participants to do the following:

- Describe the problem and the context within which it is held.
- Locate key phrases and statements within that description.
- Interpret the meaning of these phrases and statements; that is, ensure that the meanings participants give to those phrases and statements are clearly articulated.
- Identify essential or key features of the issue and the situation.
- Use this information to formulate a tentative statement that provides a sequential description of events and delineates who does what, with whom, how, when, and where.
- Check the statement with other participants, then reframe the description on the basis of their feedback.

▨ Alternative 4: Community Profile

A community profile provides a descriptive "snapshot" of the context in which the investigation is placed. It enables stakeholders to formulate an overview that describes significant features of their context. Smaller projects in restricted sites, such as classrooms, schools, community centers, and government agencies, may require information that focuses only on dimensions of the setting itself—that is, the classroom, school, agency office, and so on. In many cases, however, persistent problems require investigations that extend into the neighborhood, town, city, or region.

There is often a profusion of information about community contexts, and it is essential that the work of preparing a profile remain focused. Following preliminary activity that briefly describes the setting (see Chapter 3), researchers should ask major stakeholders for their views about the types of information pertinent to the investigation. This will help researchers choose judiciously from a potentially vast array of information and minimize the time spent amassing inconsequential information. Research facilitators should assist stakeholders in developing a community profile framework that appears most appropriate to the task at hand. A community profile might include any of the following:

- Geography: location; landforms; climate
- History: history of the setting; major events; developments; history of the problem(s) under investigation; major laws affecting the site or the problem(s)
- Government: impacts and places of local, regional, state, and federal government policies and agencies; boundaries
- Politics: parties; organizations; representatives
- Demographics: population size; gender, race, ethnic, and age distributions; births and deaths
- Economics: sectors (business and industry, etc.); employment; wages and salary levels; general status (prospering, declining)
- Health: services; agencies; facilities; special populations (e.g., older persons, children, persons with disabilities)
- Education: schools; institutions; services; sectors (e.g., primary, secondary, college); resources; community education
- Welfare: services; institutions, agencies, and organizations (government and nongovernment); personnel (social workers, counselors, etc.)

- Housing: number, type, and condition of dwellings; forms of accommodation (e.g., low rent, transient, hotel)
- Transportation: public and private transportation; accessibility and availability; areas serviced; road conditions; types (road, rail, air)
- Recreation: type, number, condition, and accessibility of facilities and services; clubs and organizations; age groups targeted
- Religion: type and number of churches; levels of attendance; activities and services
- Intergroup relations: social groups (race, ethnic, religious, or kinship affiliations); coalitions; antagonisms
- Planning: regional, city, town, or local plans

Community profiles usually provide demographic information, much of which can be gained from official or documentary sources, but information may also be acquired during preliminary observations and interviews. John Van Willigen (1993, after Vlachos, 1975) suggests a format that embodies cultural information in addition to the types of demographic data described above. The type of information collected necessarily requires extended ethnographic work with people within the setting. Van Willigen's framework incorporates *cultural tracts* that include the following:

- *Lifestyle:* economic status; communication (including language, proxemics, and expressive media); religious sites and practices; housing (styles and clustering of dwellings, place of kin networks); geographic location; institutional characteristics; health definitions and practices; education; leisure and recreational activities; politics
- *Historical features:* contemporary and historical artifacts and physical representations
- *Worldviews, beliefs, perceptions, and definitions of reality:* cognitive systems (how people think about and organize everyday reality); religious systems (spiritual reality); values systems; belief systems; perceptions of own group and others; intercultural perceptions

Once the researcher has acquired the information for the community profile, he or she can organize and present it in a form that people from all stakeholding groups can readily understand. The profile can be made available for their scrutiny as part of the process of formulating accounts (see Chapter 5). A community profile provides a structured way for participants to determine clearly the range of influences likely to have an impact on the problem under investigation. The information ensures that a broad range of relevant features of the situation are taken into account and paves the way for effective and sustainable projects and programs.

Meetings: Group Processes for Collaborative Inquiry

The working principles of community-based action research signal the need to engage processes that enable people to work together productively. Although researchers may meet informally with a variety of stakeholder groups to discuss general issues and to formulate a preliminary picture of the context in the early stages of the research process, they will need to engage more structured and formalized procedures as issues emerge. The following processes suggest the means by which research facilitators may provide structured ways to maximize participation by the diverse groups involved.

Preliminary Meetings

When diverse stakeholder groups are brought together, it is sometimes necessary, particularly when there has been a history of conflict, for researchers to do some preliminary work to ensure harmonious and productive meetings. Holding prior meetings with each of the conflicting parties can enable them to define their own agendas and to clarify the purposes of the larger meeting. In these contexts, researchers should work to formulate statements that are nonjudgmental and nonblaming yet that clearly articulate participants' perceptions and concerns.

> When I worked on community projects, I always indicated the need for joint action to people in various stakeholding groups. After I had established contact with individuals and groups and provided them with opportunities to express their viewpoints, I would signal the possibility of linking with others. I would comment that "there are a number of other people [or groups] who are concerned with this issue. It might be useful to meet with them to discuss it."

A common mistake of researchers intent on community-based action is to call a "public meeting" to discuss issues and formulate plans. Often, such meetings are held in places—schools, universities, agency offices—that are alien to many stakeholders. In consequence, many groups are poorly represented, and the organizers become disconcerted by the apparent apathy of the people they wish to engage. School principals, social workers, and health workers, for instance, cannot understand why certain parent groups will not come to meetings called specifically to deal with their children's problems. They frequently comment in these circumstances on the parents' "lack of interest" and fail to perceive how threatening formal or official environments can be for some people.

> I have been involved in many situations in which parents, especially those from lower socioeconomic environments, perceive schools and government offices as threatening and judgmental bastions of authority. Meetings held in institutional arenas often reinforce these perceptions, as articulate and self-confident people hold the floor and determine the course of events and the texts—resolutions, statements, records, and so on—that finally emerge. Persons who are less articulate are effectively silenced, their concerns unheard and their agendas unmet.

In some instances, public meetings provide contexts in which individuals or groups in conflict meet for the first time. Without preliminary work, these types of meetings may degenerate into conflict-laden situations that serve only to reinforce antagonisms and exacerbate existing problems. Public meetings, therefore, should be used only after the various stakeholder groups have had the opportunity to meet in safe and comfortable contexts to explore their issues and to clarify their thoughts and perceptions. This is imperative when large organizations and institutions provide the context for a project.

Forms of Meetings

In larger projects, researchers may work through three phases of group activity: intragroup circles, intergroup meetings, and formal working parties or committees. Smaller projects, however, often require only informal gatherings to initiate research processes.

Intragroup circles are relatively informal gatherings that enable single-interest stakeholder groups to discuss their problems and describe their situational contexts. Circles may meet in homes, offices, cafés, or other relatively small places and can take several forms:

- *Focus groups,* where people with similar interests or agendas discuss particular issues
- *In-group forums,* where people from single-interest or stakeholder groups discuss particular issues
- *Informal meetings* that form spontaneously in response to particular circumstances or issues
- *Agency, institution, or departmental meetings* that provide personnel with opportunities to discuss common interests or agendas
- *Community group meetings,* where community members meet to explore interests or agendas

Intergroup meetings enable diverse stakeholder groups to meet together to discuss issues and formulate joint constructions. They usually take place in meeting halls, conference rooms, community centers, or similar public places and generally take one of the following forms:

- *Public forums,* which explore particular issues
- *Public meetings,* which explore sets of related issues

- *Colloquiums,* which provide for extended exploration of issues
- *Conferences,* which provide contexts for extended exploration of sets of related issues

Formal Committees

A research process may require structured ways of implementing plans and proposals as it develops momentum. In these contexts, it may be appropriate to constitute formal or semiformal officially sanctioned committees. These may include the following:

- *Working parties,* which meet to deal with specific tasks
- *Steering groups,* which organize structures and processes to manage agendas identified at meetings
- *Agency or departmental special-purpose committees,* which deal with specific issues
- *Community committees,* which provide contexts for handling specific issues and/or links with relevant agencies
- *Interagency or interdepartmental committees,* which coordinate the activities of a number of agencies or departments

Organizing Meetings

Meetings don't "just happen"; careful planning and preparation must take place to ensure that participants can work through their issues and attain their objectives without the distractions of poorly articulated activities, inadequate materials and equipment, or conditions that are uncomfortable or irritating. Some of the critical issues that research facilitators need to take into account when organizing meetings are discussed below.

Participants

Meetings should reflect the participatory intent of community-based action research; it is important, therefore, to ensure that people who can legitimately speak for the interests of each stakeholding group attend. Having one or two persons represent a diverse ethnic group, for instance, may ignore the deep divisions that lie among various families, cliques, and social class groupings within that population. Researchers should review their initial social analysis to confirm that all groups are appropriately represented by individuals who can legitimately take on the role of spokesperson. Meeting conditions—time, place, and transportation—should maximize the opportunities these people have to attend.

Leadership or Facilitation

A meeting is best led by a neutral chair or facilitator—a person perceived as having no overriding loyalty to any particular stakeholding group. Researchers can act as facilitators, but it may be appropriate in some circumstances for a respected community member to act in this role. It is important that the chair or facilitator be accepted by participants as a legitimate or appropriate person to direct proceedings. Only in exceptional circumstances, for example, would a meeting investigating women's issues have a male chair.

The task of negotiating diverse perspectives in a research process can become difficult if strong and determined people try to impose their own agendas and perspectives. The chair or facilitator should employ judicious, diplomatic, yet firm processes to ensure that such people do not stifle the diverse agendas and perspectives that are essential components of the process. Researchers should, therefore, ensure that the chair or facilitator has the formal authority and the procedural skills to maintain the integrity of the meeting process. A formal statement, written or verbal, that acknowledges the chair/facilitator's authority should be obtained from key stakeholders prior to the commencement of the meeting. This may take the form of a letter or memorandum to participants or may be included in a welcoming speech at the meeting.

Significant differentials of power between the research facilitator and other participants are not conducive to productive meetings. Researchers should ensure that people of appropriate status are engaged to facilitate or lead meetings.

I was told of a situation in which an inexperienced junior professor and a graduate assistant were asked to facilitate a workshop at a conference of senior educational administrators. Within a short time, some of the administrators had marginalized the professor and graduate assistant and had taken control of the proceedings.

Ground Rules and Agenda

Researchers may ask groups in advance to suggest ground rules for meetings to minimize the possibility of conflict and to provide conditions conducive to productive work. Meeting procedures should be planned carefully to minimize the possibility that they may degenerate into heated debate, accusation, and blaming. Each meeting should begin with the presentation of a broad agenda that includes statements about (a) the purpose of the meeting, (b) the manner in which the meeting will proceed, and (c) the activities in which participants will engage. Time may be allocated for people to comment on the agenda and to suggest alternative procedures. These preliminary activities, however, should not take so much time that they detract from the main activities of the meeting.

I once attended a 1-day workshop in which 2 of the 6 available hours were expended on establishing ground rules and formulating an agenda. This use of the available time created a great deal of frustration among many of the participants because the time remaining was insufficient to deal with the intended workshop agenda.

Procedures

Meeting procedures can ensure that each group has an equal opportunity to express perceptions and concerns and to have them included in the meeting's generated statements and accounts. By making frequent use of small-group processes, facilitators can provide opportunities for people to articulate their thoughts and ideas in safety. This ensures that multiple perspectives are elicited and that forceful people do not dominate proceedings. In one useful type of small-group process, the facilitator or meeting leader follows these steps:

- Divide the meeting into groups of, usually, no more than six members.
- Describe the activities to be performed or the questions to be discussed (these may be selected from any of the frameworks for developing descriptive accounts presented in this chapter).
- Provide adequate time for these purposes to be achieved.
- Have each group write a summary of activity outcomes on a chart.
- Have all participants reassemble and display their charts.
- Have each group present its summary verbally. As each group presents, questions from the facilitator or audience may allow group members to clarify meanings and in some cases extend their descriptions. This additional information may then be added to the chart.

A number of books are available that provide useful guidance for small-group processes. One recent publication by John Gastil (1993) provides procedures consonant with the principles of community-based action research.

Decision Making

Meetings should operate on the basis of consensus, rather than on the basis of a majority vote. The latter encourages competitive, divisive politicking, which usually ensures that the least powerful groups will not have their interests met. Although consensus is sometimes difficult to attain, it is a powerful instrument for change when it is achieved. When agendas are pushed through to accommodate time pressures, bureaucratic pressures, or the interests of powerful groups, the outcomes are likely, in the long run, to be unproductive. Time is an essential element in any collaborative activity; it cannot be compressed without damaging the essential participatory nature of a community-based action research process.

Venues

Initial meetings may be held in people's homes, cafés, offices, community centers, or any other venue where the stakeholder group itself is comfortable. When people talk in the comfort of their own territory, they are more likely to be honest and forthcoming. Public venues are appropriate when all stakeholder groups meet to work through issues and agendas. Even then, however, researchers should take care to select meeting sites where the least powerful groups will feel comfortable. If a meeting is held in their territory, they are more likely both to attend and to be willing to contribute to the proceedings. A local community hall, church halls, hostels, community health clinics, lodge halls, and even parks may provide appropriate contexts.

Accounts and Reports

Two major issues inform the construction of reports and accounts. First, it is essential that accounts reflect the perceptions of all stakeholding groups. If they are written from the perspective of a limited group of stakeholders, they will provide no basis for effective and sustainable action. Accounts, therefore, are best formulated collaboratively.

Second, except in small contexts, all stakeholders usually cannot be included in the processes all the time. In these circumstances, researchers should ensure that all stakeholders are regularly informed of activities as they progress and that they have opportunities to read accounts as they are formulated (rather than at the completion of the process) and to provide feedback. This type of information may be distributed as a series of reports to the members of all stakeholder groups at regular intervals, at significant points in the research process, or both.

The processes for developing collaborative accounts are described in detail in Chapter 5. Joint descriptive accounts are derived from the following:

- Information acquired by researchers during preliminary interviews and observations
- Activities that help the members of each stakeholder group clarify their own definition of the situation
- Information gathered by researchers from other sources, including documents and interviews

Accounts result from collaborative work in which all stakeholding groups (or representatives of all stakeholding groups) define the content, form, and major features (key elements) that will be used to portray their situation.

An essential feature of this process is that it is publicly recorded in written form and accessible to all stakeholders. Descriptive accounts may be written as reports that summarize the outcomes of meetings and provide a starting point for the analytic or reflective activity that follows.

BOX 4.1
Look: Building the Picture

PURPOSE:

To assist stakeholding groups to build a picture that leads to:

Understanding	What and how events occur
Clarity	A detailed picture of the context
Insight	An extended understanding of the issue

PROCESS:

Gather information

Interviews	Key people from each stakeholding group
Observation	Significant settings, events, and/or activities
Review	Documents, records, and materials

Record information

Notes	A written record of what people said and/or did
Audiotapes	Audio record of interviews
Videotapes	Video record of events, people, places, etc.
Photographs	Photographs of events, people, places, etc.

Analyze information

Identify key elements	Identify significant items of information
Formulate categories	Group similar items
Formulate themes	Group similar categories

Construct reports

Using themes as headings, categories as subheadings, and key elements as content, construct an account for each stakeholding group that describes

Research activities	Who has done what, where, when, and why
The situation/context	Group members' descriptions
The issue	Group members' experiences and perspectives

Communicate

Inform people of research activities by distributing reports as

Meeting minutes	For meeting participants
Bulletins	For stakeholding groups
Interim reports	For key stakeholders

Think

INTERPRETING AND
ANALYZING

Chapter 4 focused on activities that help research participants clarify problems and describe the contexts within which those problems are embedded. Stakeholder groups may engage in this early activity separately to elucidate their own perspectives and their own experience. Research facilitators should bring people together as soon as this process is under way, so that all stakeholding groups together may develop a common vision that provides them with the basis for taking significant action on the issue or problem investigated. In this chapter, I describe the next part of the process, in which stakeholders interpret the information they have gathered to (a) construct reports extending their understanding of *what* is happening and *how* it is happening and (b) develop *jointly constructed reports* that interpret and explain the problems under investigation.

I begin with a brief discussion of the purpose of interpretation and then present a selection of frameworks that assist research participants to formulate interpretations of issues investigated. The chapter provides a set of procedures for developing and presenting interpretive accounts, which provide the basis for the problem-solving actions delineated in Chapter 6.

Interpretation: Clarifying Meaning

Denzin (1989) has written of the need to make the problematic, lived experience of ordinary people directly available to policymakers, welfare workers, and other service professionals, so that programs and services can be made more relevant to people's lives. He suggests that an interpretive perspective identifies different definitions of the situation, the assumptions held by various interested parties, and appropriate points of intervention:

> Research of this order can produce meaningful descriptions and interpretations of social process. It can offer explanations of how certain conditions came into existence and persist. Interpretive research can also furnish the basis for realistic proposals concerning the improvement or removal of certain events, or problems. (p. 23)

The task of the research facilitator in this phase of the research process is to interpret and render understandable the problematic experiences being considered. Interpretation builds on description through conceptual frameworks—definitions and frameworks of meaning—that enable participants to make better sense of their experiences. It uses experience-near concepts drawn from people's day-to-day lives (rather than, e.g., theoretical concepts from the behavioral sciences) to clarify and untangle meanings and to help the individuals illuminate and organize their experiences. The researcher must provide the opportunity, in other words, for participants to understand their own experiences in terms that make sense to them.

Interpretive activity exposes the conceptual structures and pragmatic working theories that people use to explain their conduct. The researcher's task is to assist participants in revealing those taken-for-granted meanings and reformulating them into "constructions [that are] improved, matured, expanded and elaborated" and that enhance their conscious experiencing of the world (Guba & Lincoln, 1989). These new ways of interpreting the situation are not intended as merely intellectualized, rational explanations; rather, they are real-life constructs-in-use that assist people in reshaping their lives.

Because diverse perspectives exist in any situation, an action research process ensures that members of each stakeholding group can comprehend the interpretations of other groups with whom they are working. Participants learn about language that is relevant to other groups, biographies that reveal other stakeholders' experiences and perspectives, and relationships within and between each of the stakeholder groups.

"Interpretation is a clarification of meaning. Understanding is the process of interpreting, knowing, and comprehending the meaning that is felt, intended, and expressed by another" (Denzin, 1989, p. 120). The purpose of interpretive work, therefore, is to help participants to "take the attitude of the other" (Mead, 1934), not in a superficial, mechanistic sense but in a way that enables them to understand empathetically the complex and deeply rooted forces that move their lives.

In some instances, initial interpretive work provides the basis for immediate action. Some problems, however, are more intransigent and require extended processes of exploration, analysis, and theorizing. The form of analysis should be appropriate to the problem at hand. Complex or highly abstract theories, when applied to small, localized issues, are likely to drain people's energy and inhibit action. Explanations and interpretations produced in action research processes should be framed in terms that participants use in their everyday lives, rather than in terms derived from the academic disciplines or professional practices.

When I began working at the community level, I would often present explanations for problems derived from my background in the social sciences. I would include concepts such as social class, racism, power, authority, and so on. In few instances did these forms of analysis strike a chord with the people with whom I was working.

On one occasion, I presented an analysis to a group of Aboriginal people that implied that their responses to racism were inappropriate. My explanation outlined a theory of minority responses to racism that highlighted apathy, avoidance, and aggression as typical behaviors that derived from a history of oppression. The anger directed at me by the Aboriginal people present was a humbling experience.

In retrospect, I understand their anger and wonder at my naïveté. Not only was I interpreting their situation from my perspective, but I was judging their behavior in stereotypical ways, implicitly criticizing their responses to situations they faced. Today, I ensure that any analysis I make is drawn from terms known to the people with whom I am working, is expressed in their language, and is derived from their experience-near concepts. My own role in this process is to assist them in articulating their ideas and to ensure that they are expressed clearly and accurately. I also ask probing questions that challenge the rigor of their interpretations to ensure that they will hold up in the court of public scrutiny and future action.

The use of experience-near concepts does not eliminate the need for rigorous inquiry. Restricted or cursory analyses that produce superficial solutions to deep-seated and complex problems are unlikely to be effective. Researchers and facilitators can ensure that explanatory frameworks are sufficiently rigorous to move people past stereotypical or simplistic interpretations of their situations, but they must be grounded in the reality of their everyday lives. They must acknowledge the experiences and perspectives of those to whom programs and services are directed, rather than of those who deliver those services.

I often hear teachers and school administrators criticizing parents, especially those in poorer circumstances, for "lack of interest in their children." They frequently comment that the parents do not participate in school programs or respond to requests to help with their children's schoolwork. School authorities often fail to recognize the deep-seated fear or mistrust felt by many poorer parents toward people in positions of authority, or the extent of their alienation from schools that results from their own educational experiences, and see any failure of parents to interact with the school as "lack of interest in their children." My experience suggests that it is possible to get past this apparent apathy only by formulating contexts in which parents and those in authority can engage in dialogue and interaction on a more or less equal basis.

Extending Understanding:
Frameworks for Interpretation

In previous phases of the research process, participants focused on describing their experience of the issue and the contexts where they live and work. The move at this stage was to ensure that they develop clear pictures of what is happening, who is involved, and how events are played out. The complexity of the issue quickly becomes evident, however, and people need structured processes to enable them to make sense of the chaotic complexity that sometimes emerges from investigations of complex issues. They need, in other words, systematic procedures that assist them in extending their understanding.

Four alternative approaches or frameworks that assist stakeholders in this process of sense-making and clarification are presented below: *interpretive questions, organizational review, concept mapping,* and *problem analysis.* Larger or more complex projects may require more extended and detailed frameworks, such as those found in the literature on management, planning, community development, and/or applied anthropology (e.g., Black, 1991; Van Willigen, 1993; Whyte, 1984).

The processes described below can help participants formulate interpretations of the problems under investigation and identify significant sources, features, and/or characteristics of the issue under investigation. These processes should be incorporated into a set of activities described in the following section, "Group Processes for Interpreting Issues."

Alternative 1: Interpretive Questions:
Why, What, How, Who, Where, When

For relatively simple projects, participants might work through a series of questions that enables them to extend their understanding of the problems and contexts they have previously described. Interpretive statements that result from this process should help them develop *explanations* that reveal the nature of the problem at hand and important features of the context that sustain it. Interpretive questions might include the following:

- Why are we meeting? (purpose, focus, problem)
- What are the key elements and features of the problem?
- How is the problem affecting us? What is happening?
- Who is being affected?
- Where are they being affected?
- When are they being affected?

It may be useful for the facilitator to repeat each of these questions a number of times to enable participants to build more information into their interpretations.

More complex projects may require more detailed and extended questioning strategies, to reveal such elements as the following:

- The history of the situation—how it came about
- The individuals, groups, and types of actors involved
- Interactions and/or relationships among the people involved
- The purposes and intents of the people involved
- The sequence and duration of related events and activities
- The attitudes and values of the people involved
- The availability of and access to resources, and their use

The following types of questions may be relevant:

- Who?
  Who is centrally involved? (individuals, groups)
  Who else is significant?
  Who are the influential people? What is the nature of their influence?
  Who is linked to whom? In what ways?
  Who is friendly or cooperative? With whom?
  Who is antagonistic or uncooperative? With whom?
  Who has resources? Which ones?

- What?

  What major activities, events, or issues are relevant to the problem?

  What is each person or group doing, or not doing?

  What are their interests and concerns?

  What are their purposes? What do they want to achieve? What
  do they want to happen?

  What do they value?

  What resources are available? (people, material, equipment, space,
  time, funds)

  What resources are being used? By whom?

- How?

  How do acts, activities, and events happen?

  How are decisions made?

  How are resources used?

  How are individuals and/or groups related to each other?

  How do different individuals and groups affect the situation?

  How much influence do they have?

- Where?

  Where do people live, meet, work, and interact?

  Where are resources located?

  Where do activities and events happen?

- When?

  When do things happen?

  When are resources available?

  When do people meet, work, and engage in activities?

  When does the problem occur?

  What is the duration of occurrences of the problem?

Not all these questions will be relevant to any one situation. The
questions the facilitator selects will depend on the context of the problem and the setting. Answers to the questions should be recorded in
detail and a summary written on a chart that can be seen by all members
of the group. Such charts help participants visualize the situation they

are interpreting and provide records that can be employed in subsequent activities.

▨ Alternative 2: Organizational Review

In some circumstances—where, for instance, different sections of the same institution or agency experience similar problems—it may be appropriate for the researcher to conduct a review of the whole organization. This activity is intended to reveal different interpretations of problematic features of the organization and sources of the problems. It is intended not as an evaluation of competence or assessment of performance but as a method for discovering points where action can be taken. Participants in the review process should focus on the following features of the organization:

- Vision and mission
  Vision: What is the overarching or general purpose of the organization? Education? Health improvement? Assistance for the needy?
  Mission: In which ways does the organization seek to enact its vision? Providing educational services, courses, and classes? Engaging in health promotion programs? Providing welfare services?

- Goals and objectives
  Goals: How does the organization seek to achieve its purposes? In what activities does it engage?
  Objectives: What are the desired outcomes of these activities? For whom?

- Structure of the organization
  Roles: Are roles clearly delineated? Who works with whom? Who has authority over whom? Who supervises and gives directions? To whom?
  Responsibilities: What types of people are responsible for different categories of activities? Who performs which types of tasks?

Rules and procedures: Is it clear what needs to be done and how it is to be done?

Resources: Are the resources required for tasks adequate and available (e.g., time, materials, and skills)?

- Operation

  Is each person clear about his or her roles and responsibilities?

  How effectively is each person enacting his or her roles and responsibilities?

  What factors hinder the enacting of those responsibilities (e.g., lack of materials, time, skills, or support)?

  Are there tasks and responsibilities to which no one is clearly assigned?

  What is not happening that should be? What is happening that should not be? Where are the gaps? Where are the barriers?

- Problems, issues, and concerns

  What problems, issues, and concerns are expressed by stakeholders?

  Who is associated with each?

  How do stakeholders explain or interpret problems, issues, and concerns?

As participants work through these issues, they will extend their understanding of the organization and aspects of its operation that are relevant to their problems, issues, and concerns. The outcomes of their inquiries should be recorded in detail and summarized on charts for use in later stages of the research process.

I once worked as a consultant with a community child care agency whose mandate was to find appropriate foster homes for children and to ensure that those families were adequately supported. The agency was experiencing a number of difficulties in performing these functions. Staff members were stressed and overworked, and funding sources questioned the effectiveness of the agency's services. When we charted the purposes for which the agency had been formed and matched those against its actual activities, we discovered that staff were engaged in work that was of peripheral relevance to the agency's stated main function. They were attempting to provide a wide range of support services to foster families—furniture, clothing, food, and counseling— that could be provided by other agencies funded for those purposes. When they saw what was happening, staff and committee members decided to terminate many of those activities and to link clients to other relevant agencies when such needs arose.

▨ Alternative 3: Concept Mapping

Long-term, deep-seated problems frequently defy the remedial efforts of professional practitioners. Occurrences of drug abuse, eating disorders, alienation from schoolwork, youth crime, and other problems are so pervasive that they often appear beyond the reach of ordinary programs and services. They exist as part of a complex system of interwoven events and circumstances that are deeply embedded in the social fabric of the community.

Attempts to remediate these problems are unlikely to be successful if they focus merely on one aspect of the interrelated factors that make up the situation. Quick-fix, spray-on solutions rarely work. Participants need to reconceptualize such issues in ways that clearly identify the interrelationships among all the significant elements that affect the situation. The intent of this type of activity is to help participants find a way to pursue multiple, holistic, and inclusive strategies that will assist people in dealing with the problems that affect their lives.

In the first phase of the research process, delineated in Chapter 4, participants described the problem and defined key elements or characteristics of the situation. In concept mapping, those elements are plotted diagrammatically, so that participants can visualize the ways in which different components of the situation relate to the problems they are investigating. To guide participants in formulating a concept map, the facilitator should take the following steps:

- Begin by printing on a large piece of paper or a board visible to all participants a word or phrase that characterizes the central

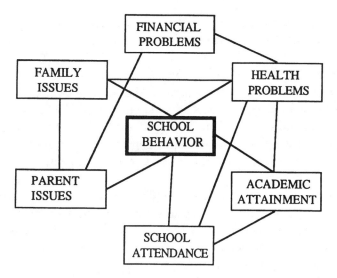

Figure 5.1. Concept Map of Poor School Behavior

problem, and then enclose the word or phrase inside a geometric figure (e.g., square or circle).

- Add to the chart other geometric figures labeled to represent various elements associated with the problem.
- Link the figures containing the elements that seem to be related to each other.
- Extend the mapping process to include additional figures until all participants are satisfied that all significant elements have been included.

An example of a concept map is provided in Figure 5.1. This interpretation of poor school behavior of youth in a rural town is ascribed by stakeholders to a number of interlinked factors—poor attendance, low academic attainment, general family issues, parent issues, financial problems, and poor health. All issues are seen to contribute to the identified behavior problem and need to be addressed as part of the process of defining a solution to the problem of poor school behavior. Further analysis may have extended this map to delineate factors associated with health problems, financial problems, and so on.

Financial problems, for instance, may be associated with high unemployment in the town, which in turn may relate to closure of businesses or other economic conditions.

Concept maps help participants visualize the major influences that need to be taken into account and assist them in evaluating whether all relevant stakeholders have been included in the investigation. In Figure 5.1, the appearance of "family issues" signals the need to involve relevant family members in the inquiry process. The young people who are themselves the focus of the problem should be central to the concept-mapping process.

Incorporating additional stakeholders may extend, in turn, the factors incorporated into the map and, therefore, the elements that need to be considered when action is planned. This form of analysis can be further expanded by including activities from other interpretive frameworks (e.g., interpretive questions).[1]

The explanatory frameworks produced in this process are not meant to be scientifically or professionally defensible. We are looking not for the "best" or the "correct" explanation but for one that makes sense to or can be accommodated by all the stakeholders. In all the processes described above, it is essential that each stakeholding group provide input about its own situation. Analyses based on other people's interpretations do not provide an appropriate basis for action. In Figure 5.1, for instance, teacher or administrator perspectives on the family are less relevant than the perspectives of the family members themselves. Outsider interpretations often are incomplete or inaccurate and are sometimes judgmental; they may tend to create divisiveness and hostility, which are antithetical to the participatory principles of community-based action research.

▒ Alternative 4:
Problem Analysis:
Antecedents and Consequences

An approach similar to concept mapping enables participants to identify the antecedents of existing problems (i.e., elements of the situation that led up to the problems) and the consequences that derive from those problems. In this process, the facilitator should have each stakeholder group identify the following elements and describe them on a chart:

- The core problem
- Major antecedents to the problem
- Other significant factors related to those antecedents
- Major negative consequences
- Other significant consequences

A committee of agency workers and community representatives investigated the high incidence of juvenile crime in a small country town. A process of exploration revealed that criminal activity appeared to be related to the lack of leisure activities for teenagers and to poor school attendance. No one in town accepted responsibility for organizing activities, there were few facilities available for that purpose, and the school provided little in the way of after-school programs or activities. Poor school attendance was directly related to poor school performance, uninteresting or irrelevant curricula, and family poverty.

As a result of increases in juvenile crime—burglary, petty theft, and vandalism—there was a general increase in alienation of some groups of young people from other sectors of the community. There were increasing incidents of conflict between youth and members of the community—businesspeople, law enforcement personnel, teachers, and so on—and a deterioration in employment opportunities for young people. The long-term prospects of some youth also seemed likely to be affected by the negative outcomes of incarceration in prisons and other institutions and growing criminal records. This situation is drawn as a concept map in Figure 5.2.

This process is sometimes defined as "causes" and "effects," rather than antecedents and consequences. In many situations, however, it is impossible to delineate the difference between cause and effect

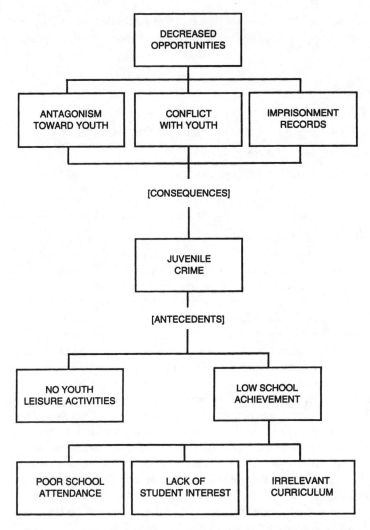

Figure 5.2. Antecedents and Consequences of Juvenile Crime

because of the complexity of interactions between the constituent parts of the picture. The same phenomena often can be envisaged as cause, effect, or both. Nevertheless, this approach can help participants identify significant elements of their analysis and visualize aspects of the situation that require action.

Group Processes for Interpreting Issues

In this phase of the investigation, researchers assist participants to engage in discussion and dialogue—hermeneutic dialectic processes—with the intent of developing mutually acceptable accounts that extend their understanding of the issues and problems they are investigating. Interpretive activities may take place within meetings in which descriptive accounts are formulated or may require a separate gathering if the process is more complex. The same rules apply, however. Members of all stakeholder groups should feel themselves to be represented adequately and that their agendas and perspectives are included as significant parts of the process. Researchers assist participants to organize meetings, set an agenda, review descriptive accounts, develop and analyze interpretive accounts, and formulate follow-up activities. Detailed procedures for each of these steps follow.

Organizing Meetings

Research facilitators will work with key stakeholders to organize meetings. It is important that members of the principal stakeholding group, that for whom the problem or issue is most central, have a key role to play in the organization of meetings. They should ensure that representatives who can speak for each of the stakeholding groups are able to attend the meetings.

Procedures for organizing meetings were presented in Chapter 4. Those responsible for organizing meetings will need to take account of participants, meeting facilitation, agendas, procedures, decision-making processes, and venues. The time required for these processes will vary according to the complexity of the issues and the number of groups involved. It may involve a workshop lasting a day or a few days or may require a series of meetings for a time.

▓▓▓ **Procedures for Interpreting Issues**

Setting the Agenda

In this phase of the process, participants learn something about the *people* involved, the *purpose* of meeting, and the *activities* in which they will be engaged. The facilitator's role includes the following duties:

- Inform people of the purpose of the meeting.
- Provide an opportunity for participants to introduce themselves and identify the groups to which they belong.
- Present a broad agenda for the session.
- Allow time for participants to discuss, clarify, and modify the agenda. Do not discuss the *issues* at this time but focus on the processes of the meeting.

Reviewing Descriptive Information

The purpose of this activity is to give participants a chance to review the descriptive information produced in previous meetings. This is especially important when stakeholding groups have done some initial work separately. Facilitators should provide opportunities for each stakeholding group to do the following:

- Send written versions of the descriptive accounts or give them to participants prior to the meeting.
- Present a verbal report that summarizes descriptive information produced by their previous activities.
- Present the key elements of these reports on a chart.

Facilitators should allow time for meeting participants to discuss and clarify the accounts, avoiding extended or detailed discussion unless there are contentious issues that need to be resolved.

Distilling the Information: Analysis

By this stage of the process, a great deal of information may have been produced. Participants will work with this information to identify salient sets of ideas, concepts, or issues and condense them into categories that provide the basis for further action. Participants should work collectively to organize the information in the charted summaries into sets of categories. They should identify *converging perspectives* (i.e., those ideas, concepts, or elements common to all or a number of groups) and *diverging perspectives* (i.e., those ideas, concepts, or elements found in the accounts of only one or a few groups). Because this activity is time-consuming, it may sometimes be appropriate to formulate a *working party* to carry it out:

- Participants should select elements from the charts that are perceived to be significant features or characteristics of the issue investigated.

- Participants should sort elements into categories, so that those associated in some significant way are clustered together. The idea is to rationalize the large number of individual ideas, accounts, or issues to create a smaller number of categories. In doing so, facilitators should ensure that the process of categorizing does not erase important information. A category labeled "youth issues," for instance, might erase important distinctions between early and late teens, or between males and females. Decisions about ideas that can be incorporated into particular categories and those that must remain separate should be made through discussion and negotiation.

- Participants may organize categories in a variety of ways. A color coding system may be used, for example, wherein similar items are identified on charts with colored markers. Alternatively, each idea, issue, or concept may be copied onto a card, and the cards can then be sorted into piles according to their similarities or common characteristics. Groups have also used large-sized "stick-it" labels, placing all elements on a large wall and allowing participants move them around to groups associated together. Participants should know that there is no right way or correct answer for this process. The way that they organize the information is the way that makes best sense to them collectively.

- When participants have reached agreement on the categories and the information contained in each, they should classify each

Information from Reports 10.10.99

Identified Categories

CHILDREN

TEACHERS

PLAY

SCHOOL

Figure 5.3. Example: Issues Derived From Categorized Information

group of concepts according to a label or term that both identifies and describes the category. This process is represented symbolically in Figure 5.3.

Extending People's Understanding: Frameworks for Interpretation

Having identified the major issues (contained in the categories from the previous activity), participants will next work to extend their understanding of the issue(s) investigated. Facilitators should select an appropriate set of activities from the "Frameworks for Interpretation" detailed in previous sections of this chapter: interpretive questions, organizational review, concept mapping, or problem analysis. The following should be kept in mind when working within any of these frameworks.

- Participants should review the list of issues (categories).
- Participants should prioritize the issues in order of importance or significance. In this process, ensure that the perspectives of principal stakeholding participants are taken into account.

- Participants should organize themselves into groups, each containing no more than six participants drawn from different stakeholding groups.
- Each group will be given responsibility for one of the prioritized issues. If there are few issues, then more than one group may work on an issue. Groups should be kept small so that all people have an opportunity to talk to the issue.
- Facilitators should explain the purpose and sequence of activities for the chosen framework for interpretation (e.g., "Concept Mapping").
- Adequate time should be allowed for each group to proceed through the activities.
- Outcomes of the activity must be acceptable to all group members.
- Groups should summarize the outcomes of their activity on charts.

Presenting Interpretive Accounts

At this point, each small group will present the outcome of the above activities to the larger gathering:

- Groups will display all charts.
- Each group will present a verbal synopsis of the charted information. Wherever possible, several group members should participate in this activity. When presentation is provided by an individual representative, the representative should ensure that the summary is acceptable by asking other members whether significant information has been overlooked.
- As each group presents its account, other participants may ask questions. This will help group members clarify or extend their statements. Extra information derived from this process should be added to the charted summary.

Identifying Priorities for Action

Participants will identify those issues or agendas that require action most urgently and therefore have the highest priority, using the following steps:

- Review major elements of experience on charts.
- Identify agendas requiring action.
- Identify priorities for action: Identify common or related agendas, identify unique agendas, and list in order of priority.

Formulating Follow-Up Activities

In the final phase, participants arrange follow-up activities and conclude the session. Facilitators provide participants with opportunities to do the following:

- *Debrief,* or comment on the session's activities.
- *Plan the next phase of the process,* developing a joint account using input from participants (What do we need to do next? How will we do it?).
- *Designate a working party* that includes representation from each stakeholding group and arrange a time and place for the working party to meet.
- *Celebrate the group's accomplishments in some tangible way,* with a song, handshakes all around, congratulations, or whatever else might fit the occasion.

Constructing Joint Reports

The process described above results in significant information that will form the basis for actions to be taken by participants. It is important that the outcomes of workshops are recorded and presented in report form to all stakeholders so that people are informed of and feel included in the continuing processes of development. Research facilitators should promptly organize a meeting with the working party to formulate a report. At the meeting, facilitators should take the following steps:

- Greet working party participants and present an agenda that includes the purpose of the meeting and a list of the activities in which they will engage.
- Review materials from the meetings/workshops.

- Assist working party members in using key elements from meetings/workshops to outline a report (see sections on reporting in previous chapters and in Chapter 8).
- Check the final outline with participants.

Subsequent to the meeting, facilitators should engage in the following activities:

- Use the outline to write a detailed written account. Detailed records from meetings should provide the content of the report.
- Forward a copy of the account to all members of the working party and provide an opportunity for each of them to give feedback.
- Modify the report on the basis of their comments.
- Meet again with the working party if any members suggest significant revisions.
- Distribute the report to all stakeholders.

Presentations and Performances

In his book *Interpretive Ethnography,* Norman Denzin (1997) signals the need for forms of reporting that more clearly are able to represent people's lived experience. Current formats tend to render people's lives in forms that are stiff, formalistic, and often encompassed in technical language. They silence the voices of people to whom they refer and mask the realities of their day-to-day lives. Denzin suggests the need for reports that are more evocative, enabling readers to more readily understand people's experiences. Such reports would be open-ended, would be many sited, would not indulge in abstract terminology, would be multivoiced, and would not privilege the perspective of persons in positions of authority. Thus he suggests the need for writing that experiments with genre, voice, and narrative style, so that "official" reports may take on the appearance of writing more usually associated with fiction or poetry.

He extends this argument to suggest that such writing may be envisaged as "texts waiting to be staged." That is, people may better be able to represent their ideas and experiences through performances rather than written reports. Thus it may be possible to present the outcomes of a research process as

- Drama
- Role play
- Simulation
- Dance
- Song
- Poem
- Work of art
- A combination of the above

This move to performance is especially important in action research because participants often include people whose feelings of well-being are diminished by the intrusion of formalistic texts. Researchers need to find ways of communicating that do not disempower groups of participants.

A researcher once showed me a report she had written for a government agency that presented an Aboriginal community's account of a research process in which they had engaged. I asked her how many people in the community had read the report, and she admitted that few would wish or be able to read what was rather a thick and formal report. "How," I asked her, "will people get to know about the information in the report?" because it addressed a variety of issues related to a number of groups in the community. Her first impulse was to write another version of the report, but I suggested she think of a concert. This would enable different groups to present their perspectives in ways that were more in keeping with the life of the community. Thus people could choose to use song, dance, drama, poetry, humor, role plays, or other forms of presentation to get their message across.

Modern technology opens up possibilities for communication that were not available in the past. Groups may choose, for instance, to use carefully scripted video presentations to present information in their own voice and in their own way. This form of presentation provides many dramatic and effective possibilities for communicating the outcomes of a research process.

I recently participated in a departmental review process, whereby each of the units of the department reported on their activities for the year. The administration section staff, largely younger women, were somewhat shy and loath to present personally, so they produced a video. Taped in their offices, in a swimming pool, and in the garden, all members of the administrative staff reported on their activities. Their presentations were often touched with humor, as with one woman who would speak to the camera only through a hole in a paper bag over her head. The video presentation was engaging and informative and provided other staff with a clear understanding of the work in which administrative staff were engaged and the issues that confronted them.

There are contexts and purposes, therefore, that may be better served by more creative thinking about the best ways for communicating information to audiences of stakeholders. Although formal written reports may be useful in some contexts, it is possible that more innovative uses of narrative texts, staged performances, or electronic productions may enhance the work in which we are engaged. Researchers need to keep the audience and the purpose clearly in mind as we formulate ways to communicate effectively the outcomes of our research processes.

Conclusion

The procedures described above provide the means by which people can formulate clear, sophisticated, useful explanations and interpretations of their situations. The specific ideas and concepts contained within these interpretive frameworks provide the basis for planning concrete actions to remedy the problems on which the research has focused.

For complex problems involving multiple stakeholder groups, the activities described in this chapter may be enacted as separate parts of an action research process. For simpler problems within discrete settings, such as classrooms, offices, and small organizations, they may be incorporated into processes that move more directly from description, through interpretation, to problem solving. It is well to keep the distinction between these activities in mind, however, to ensure that people are clear about the nature and purpose of the processes in which they are engaged.

As presented here, the procedures may seem long-winded and complex, but experience will show researchers when and how to consolidate or abbreviate them to ensure a brisk, purposeful flow of activity. Researchers should be wary, however, of simplifying the research process by confining it to a small inner circle or by omitting "troublesome" stakeholders. Participation boosts personal investment in the process, extends people's understanding of the contexts and social processes in which they are involved, and minimizes the possibility that the research will bog down in conflict. Community-based action research is not just a tool for solving problems; it is a valuable resource for building a sense of community.

Note

1. Deshler (1990) provides a more extensive treatment of concept mapping.

BOX 5.1
Think: Interpreting and Analyzing

PURPOSE:

To use interpretive processes to extend and clarify people's
understanding of the issue and identify priorities for action

PROCESS:

Extend participants' understanding:
Frameworks for interpretation

Interpretive questions: Why, what, how, who, where, when
Organizational review: vision, mission, structure, operation,
problems
Concept mapping: Issue, concepts/influences, links
Problem analysis: Problem, antecedents, consequences

Group processes for interpreting issues

Meet with representatives of all stakeholding groups
Set the agenda: Clarify the purpose of the meeting
Review descriptive information: Identify key elements of
experience
Distill the information: Analyze by sorting elements into
categories
Extend understanding of issues: Enact interpretive activities
described in a "Framework for Interpretation"

Identify priorities for action

Formulate follow-up activities: Identify next steps; formulate
working party

Construct joint reports

Working party: Organize meeting of stakeholder representatives
Review materials: Identify key elements from previous activities
Formulate structure of report: Arrange in appropriate sequence
of headings
Write report: Write draft, obtain feedback, write final manuscript

Act

RESOLVING THE PROBLEMS

Simple Problems, Simple Solutions

The preceding chapters have explored processes of systematic inquiry that extend stakeholders' understanding of the problems that affect their work and community lives. I have described routines that can help stakeholders describe and analyze their situations to understand the ways in which their problems are embedded in the everyday activities and practices of their work and community lives. These routines embody principles of practice that enable researchers to develop positive working relationships with community members by communicating effectively and providing opportunities for stakeholders to participate purposefully in research activities. What I have described is a community-building process that enables people to take collective action to resolve the problems and issues that affect their lives.

The previous chapter suggested ways to formulate reports of the outcomes of research processes. Reports, in whatever form, do not necessarily lead to action, so it is imperative that action research processes include clearly articulated processes for developing action related to routines and practices that are part of participants' everyday work or social lives. How, researchers should ask, can we do things differently to get better results, so that we eliminate inappropriate ways of working and formulate our professional or organizational activities in ways that are more productive and less problematic?

Key elements and categories that emerge from the interpretive processes described in the previous chapter suggest areas of professional and organizational life that require modification or adaptation. Action research processes enable participants to review their work activities, taking these elements or categories of experience into account. The concepts and issues derived from this analysis signal the areas in which changes in policies, programs, practices and procedures, and planning processes are needed. The planning processes in this chapter suggest ways for formulating new scripts that provide the basis for different ways in which these may be written and enacted.

We now turn, therefore, to processes that enable people to formulate practical solutions to the problems they perceive. As they reflect on the information derived from processes of interpretation, they have opportunities to conceive of solutions to problems with a degree of clarity often difficult to accomplish in the rush and clutter of their day-to-day lives. If research facilitators have been successful in developing productive working relationships in the early stages of the research process, the planning stage should be relatively painless.

The procedures described below are based on a framework of action that involves three phases:

- *Planning*, which involves setting priorities and defining tasks
- *Implementing the supporting, modeling, and linking* activities that help participants accomplish their tasks
- *Evaluating*, in which participants review their progress

Planning

To commence the planning phase, research facilitators should meet with all stakeholders to obtain consensus on the actions to be taken. This crucial point in the process of community-based action research is likely to have a big impact on the success of the project. If stakeholders can agree on a course of action and become engaged in activities that they see as purposeful and productive, they are likely to invest considerable time and energy in research activities, developing a sense of ownership that maximizes the likelihood of success. Action that is rushed through to satisfy a political or bureaucratic desire to show that "something is being done," on the other hand, has little chance of success.

Sorting Out Priorities

All stakeholder groups should be involved in this process. As people review the issues and formulate their priorities, facilitators should ensure that *all* voices are heard. The objective is to reach consensus about the order in which issues and concerns should be addressed. Voting procedures should be avoided, as they tend to result in win/lose processes that weaken the community-building process. If large numbers of people are involved, they can work in small, mixed groups that come together for plenary sessions that provide the context for a final resolution of priorities. At this stage, participants should do the following:

- Review previous reports or accounts.
- List issues or concerns contained in the reports.
- Organize the issues in order of priority.
- Rate the issues according to degree of difficulty (it is often best to commence with activities that are likely to be successful).

Goals, Objectives, and Tasks

Once issues and concerns have been prioritized, they can be restated as a set of goals. For example, the issue "increasing juvenile crime" might be restated as a goal: "to decrease juvenile crime." Objectives related to this goal are revealed through processes of analysis. The analysis of juvenile crime depicted in Figure 5.2 (in Chapter 5), for instance, suggests that factors related to increased juvenile crime include "lack of youth leisure activities," "poor school attendance," and "lack of after-school programs." These factors may be stated as a set of objectives: to develop youth leisure activities, to improve youth school attendance, and to organize after-school programs. Teams of relevant stakeholders should develop a plan for each issue and bring them to plenary sessions for discussion, modification (if necessary), and endorsement.

It is essential that each planning group include a member from each of the primary stakeholding groups. The issue "poor school attendance," for instance, should have a team that includes teachers, youth, school administrators, and parents.

The simple framework of asking why, what, how, who, where, and when provides the basis for a systematic planning process:

- *Why:* State why these activities are required—for example, to combat juvenile crime. (This can be defined as a goal statement that describes the broad issue to be addressed.)
- *What:* State what actions are to be taken in the form of a set of objectives—for example, to organize an after-school program for teenagers and to develop a youth center.
- *How:* Define a sequence of tasks and activities for each objective. List them step-by-step.
- *Who:* List the people who are willing to be responsible for each task and activity.
- *Where:* State where the tasks will be done.
- *When:* State when work on each task should commence and when it should be completed.

It is sometimes useful for the facilitator to create a grid in which to set out the tasks and activities to be accomplished (see Figure 6.1). Such a grid clearly defines all dimensions of the project and allows people to see their places in the broader scheme of things. It provides a concrete

TASKS	STEPS	PEOPLE	PLACE	TIME
1.	a. b. c. d.			
2.	a. b. c. d.			
3.	a. b. c. d.			

Figure 6.1. Grid for Tasks to Be Accomplished

vision of the active community of which they are a part and enables participants to check on their progress as they work through the various stages of the project together.

Once the grid is filled in, the participants can check that each issue has an action plan and that each person is clear about his or her responsibilities. They can also check the availability of material and human resources required for the tasks:

- What materials and/or equipment are needed? Who will obtain them? From where? When?
- Are funds needed? Where will they come from? Who will organize them? When?
- Does the person responsible have the time available to do the tasks?
- Should other people be involved? For what tasks? Who will ask them? How will they become part of the process? Who will describe the project to them? How can they become part of the community?

Each of these elements can be included as part of the planning process, with objectives, tasks, and activities carefully defined and assigned. Significant problems may require an extensive array of activities that require careful monitoring, but smaller projects may need only limited time and resources for planning.

I recently reviewed a university course with class participants. A briefing by the instructor provided me with a basic understanding of the major parameters of the course. I also read the course outline and scanned notes that had been provided to students (preliminary work). I then met with the class and had participants describe how the class had operated, asking probing questions to elicit more and more detail. As they talked, I summarized their descriptions, using phrases drawn from their own words, and checked to ensure their appropriateness (description).

I then divided class members into small groups and asked each group to create a list of those facets of the course the group members had enjoyed and/or found most productive and a separate list of those aspects of the course that were problematic for them or had caused them some concern. The small groups provided safe contexts that enabled the students to express themselves freely, without fear that they might individually incur the displeasure of the instructor. I asked the groups to mark with asterisks those features of the course they had listed about which there was common consent; individual concerns were listed but unmarked.

As the groups presented their lists to the whole class, I asked questions that enabled individuals to express their ideas more fully, to explain particular words and phrases in fuller terms, and to clarify their meanings. This process also provided a context in which participants could understand, through discussion and an exchange of viewpoints, the different experiences of each member of the class. These shared ideas revealed ways in which individuals could improve the quality of their participation in the class as well as ways in which the problematic features of the class might be remedied (interpretation).

As the students worked, a discernible sense of "togetherness" developed, enhancing the collaborative processes that participants had highlighted as one of the most positive aspects of the course.

In the final phase of the process, I withdrew from active involvement and watched as the instructor worked with the other participants to modify the program for the final weeks of the course. They mapped out a plan of activities that built on the strengths of the course that had been listed and modified the learning strategies and activities that had been listed as concerns (planning). Much of this process was relatively straightforward because the solutions largely had been suggested during the previous discussion. Participants had only to formalize procedures and incorporate them in a systematic, planned course of action.

▨ Quality Check

The heart of community-based action research is not the techniques and procedures that guide action but the sense of unity that holds people to a collective vision of their world and inspires them to work together for the common good. The planning processes detailed above provide a clear set of tasks and activities, but they are not complete until these activities are checked against a set of principles. The essence of this part of the planning process is not only to check that the tasks have been described adequately but to ensure that each of the participants is aware of the need to perform them in ways that are consonant with community-based processes.

Each participant should have the opportunity to discuss his or her tasks and activities, so that all describe *what* they will do and the *way* in which they will go about doing it. Facilitators should assist this process by having participants check their activities against the criteria for the well-being of the people (see Chapter 2). Each person should be asked to make sure that his or her tasks and activities are enacted in ways that will enhance the elements of human well-being:

- *Pride:* feelings of self-worth (Will these activities enhance people's images of themselves?)
- *Dignity:* feelings of autonomy, independence, and competence (Are we doing things for people instead of enabling them to do them, either by themselves or with our assistance?)

- *Identity:* affirmation of individuals' social identities (Are the right people performing the tasks? Are women, for instance, performing tasks related to women's issues?)
- *Control:* feelings of control over resources, decisions, actions, events, and activities (Can people perform the tasks in their own way?)
- *Responsibility:* people's accounting for their own actions (Are we trusting them to perform the tasks in ways that make sense to them?)
- *Unity:* the solidarity of groups of which people are members (Do they have to alienate themselves from their group to perform the tasks?)
- *Place:* places where people feel at ease (Can they do the tasks in their own places?)
- *Location:* locales to which people have historical, cultural, or social ties (Do we need to relocate some of our activities?)

Facilitators also need to check on whether their own activities are consonant with the set of principles outlined in Chapter 2:

- *Relationships:* Will the way the activities are performed
     promote feelings of *equality* for all people involved?
     maintain *harmony* and avoid conflicts? (Have we planned how
          to *resolve conflicts?*)
     encourage the *acceptance* of people as they are?
     encourage *personal, cooperative relationships?*
     encourage *sensitivity* to people's feelings?

- *Communication:* Have the researchers
     arranged to *advise* people about what is happening in ways
          that they can *understand?*
     organized activities in ways that enable them to be *truthful,
          open, and sincere?*
     checked that their activities are socially and *culturally appro-
          priate* to the context?
     provided ways for people to *comment* on the plans?
     acted on what the people have said?

- *Participation:* Have the researchers

  provided real, nontoken opportunities for people to *perform tasks*, or are they just spectators to or recipients of facilitators' "help"?

  supported people as they performed their tasks and activities?

  dealt *personally* with people rather than through intermediaries?

- *Inclusion:* Have researchers

  involved *all* stakeholding *groups?* (Are all relevant people involved?)

  planned for *all* relevant *issues* for all stakeholding groups? (Have they focused on narrow administrative or political agendas? Have they forgotten anything?)

  obtained the cooperation of all other *relevant groups, agencies, and organizations?* (Are there other groups or organizations that need to know what is being done?)

  ensured that all relevant groups *benefit* from the activities?

Reflection on these questions may require research facilitators and other participants to modify their activities or the manner in which they intend to carry them out. Participants may find that they need to delay or postpone some activities temporarily to perform some necessary preparatory work. Any modifications to the plan should be expedited because long delays can drain people's energy and enthusiasm. Time and energy spent in such extra activities often constitute a sound investment, however, because they tend to minimize delays and blockages that happen further down the line if that preparatory work is not done. The participatory and inclusive relationships enacted in community-based action research provide the benefit of a harmonious, supportive, and energizing environment that is not only personally rewarding but also productive practically.

Implementing

Community-based processes often start with a flourish. Much enthusiasm and energy are generated as plans are articulated and people set off to perform their designated tasks. The best of intentions, however, often run up against the cold, hard realities of daily life. Participants in the research process reenter family, work, and community contexts, where responsibilities and crises crowd out new activities. As participants attempt to implement the tasks that have been set, research facilitators should (a) provide the emotional and organizational support they need to keep them on track and to maintain their energy, (b) model sound community-based processes, and (c) link the participants to a supportive network.

▓ Supporting

In the early stages of activity, people often find themselves, to some extent, out on a limb. If the preliminary work has included all people affected by the research process—the stakeholders—then the performance of new tasks or different approaches to routine tasks will usually proceed with few impediments. Even so, people usually take risks when they change their usual routines and processes, and sometimes they experience criticism and disapproval. In addition, the best of plans cannot take all contingencies into account, and performing new tasks may turn out to be much more difficult than people had anticipated. To a greater or lesser extent, they will experience feelings of doubt, threat, and/or anxiety that impede their ability to continue with research activities.

In these circumstances, the press of continual work and life demands can easily lead to research tasks being delayed or neglected. The main job of the research facilitator will be to provide the practical support that will enable people to continue their research activities. Support can be provided in many ways, some of which are described briefly below.

Communication Mechanisms

Facilitators should communicate with each participant regularly and organize simple ways in which participants with similar or related tasks can communicate. Such interactions may take the form of prearranged regular visits, telephone calls, arrangements for emergency contact, and informal social contacts—meeting for lunch, a beer after work, and so on. It is important that each person be linked with others so that participants can discuss their problems, celebrate accomplishments, maintain focus, and sustain their sense of identity with the research project.

I once assisted a group of community development workers in forming a support network for themselves after they had a attended a planning conference. Because they were located in communities many hundreds of miles apart, opportunities for interaction were limited. I arranged a regular telephone conference call in which they could discuss issues, share ideas, and generally "unload." Later, each of them commented on how important that contact was. It lessened their feelings of isolation and enabled them to keep on track when other agendas and problems threatened to divert their energies.

I have also encouraged other groups to develop small support networks that can meet easily on a regular basis. Meeting for coffee, during lunch breaks, or for dinners, these groups can provide a relaxing and safe environment in which the members can talk through their problems and gain emotional support as they do so.

Personal Nurturing

As people work through their assigned tasks, their worlds are often changed in some fundamental way. They sometimes gain a deeper understanding of themselves, their need to trust both their own judgment and those around them, and the extent of the risks they are taking. In such circumstances, people often need personal reassurance and affirmations of their competence and worth. Facilitators should be constantly sensitive to the need to provide affirming comments to people engaged in research activities—not in a patronizing or mechanical way but authentically and specifically.

I recently asked a young teacher to speak to a university class about the work she was doing in her classroom. At first she hesitated, recommending that instead I ask another person who is an "expert" in the field. "Amy," I said, "I've heard you talk about your work and really like the ideas you have and the way you link them to the practical, daily realities of teaching. I think you would be much better for the job than an 'expert' who may have many good ideas but can't make the direct links you can. In addition, the young women in the class will be able to identify directly with you, because you are like them in many ways." Not only did she agree to speak to the class, she provided an excellent presentation that was applauded by class members.

Reflection and Analysis

Visits and conversations provide researchers with opportunities to ask questions that can help participants who are performing tasks describe and reflect on their activities. Such questions may touch on some of the following areas:

- *Relationships:* How have people responded to this [new] activity? Are they supportive? Has anyone caused any problems for you?

- *Patterns of work and organization:* Can you combine your activities with your work? Does this cause any problems? Do your tasks conflict with other people's ways of working?

- *Communication:* Who have you talked with about your tasks/activities? Have you talked with your supervisor/manager/administrator? Your fellow workers/teachers/clients? What have their responses been? Who would be useful to talk with from time to time? Who can support you?

- *Difficulties and solutions:* Are you having any problems? Have you overcome them?

- *Progress:* How are things working out for you? Have you made much progress? What have people been saying about your activities?

It is important that facilitators not judge the performance of the participants, even if asked to do so. There is a great difference between saying, "Things don't appear to be going very well," and asking, "How are things going for you?" Facilitators should encourage participants to review each aspect of their tasks, talking through the processes in which they are engaged and touching base on the principles, for example, "Who have you talked with about this? Will you be able to continue with this task? How are people responding to your activities?"

Assistance

When participants experience difficulties, research facilitators may need to provide assistance. They can assist directly with some activities, providing or seeking out information, doing small tasks, or acquiring needed materials. It is important that research facilitators not take over the tasks but merely provide sufficient help to enable the participant to initiate or complete them successfully. Researchers need to develop the facility to do things *with* people and not *for* them; they need to be especially wary of the temptations that arise when working with others in areas in which the researchers have expertise. It is usually more important that the people involved develop the skills to maintain the process than just that the job get done. When facilitators take over a job, they implicitly highlight the incompetence of other participants and disempower them in the process.

Conflict Resolution

Conflicts, whether minor disagreements or major arguments, are not uncommon in action research. The researcher who has maintained a relatively neutral stance in the research process can take the position of a disinterested party in a dispute. In these situations, the researcher's mediating role is to assist the parties in conflict in coming to a resolution that is satisfactory to everyone. The task is to manage the conflict so that all parties can describe their situations clearly, analyze the sources of conflict, and work toward a resolution that enables them to maintain positive working relationships.

Modeling

The ways in which research facilitators enact their supportive role will provide direct cues to other participants regarding their own ways of working. Researchers' availability and the manner in which they provide assistance and support should implicitly demonstrate community-based processes. Their openness and authenticity should illustrate the difference between a community-based approach and a patriarchal, bureaucratic, controlling style of operation.

As they work with other participants, researchers should ensure that their procedures and working styles enact the processes and principles of community-based research. Their conversations can describe their own and other people's activities, and they should find opportunities to give "gifts"—news, information, snacks, a telephone number, or a flower. As they describe their own activities, research facilitators provide information in an analytic form that demonstrates ways in which people may reflect on their own work, for example,

> I've managed to help Mary find someone who can assist her with her project. They've already been able to . . . She says that she's really starting to feel good about that and intends to . . . She feels more comfortable now that she's able to talk with the other people in her office. Next time I see her, I'll . . .

Extended discussions provide opportunities for facilitators to pass on information but also cue people to reflect on their own activities. Modeling is one of the most powerful means of instituting the social processes that are inherent in community-based research. The doing is worth much more than the saying.

I recently taught a successful graduate course called Community-Based Ethnography. Of all the student feedback I received, the most consistent comments related to the way in which I taught the course. One student noted, "The instructor not only teaches about community-based research; he does it."

A member of a community in which I worked once criticized a consultant who had failed to live up to his expectations. "He can talk the talk," he said, "but he can't walk the walk."

▓ Linking

A support network is a key ingredient in the success of a project. This is true not only for the research process itself but for each of the participants involved. As people plan their tasks and activities, they can nominate the people who are likely to support them and take steps to establish relationships with them. Participants will do much of this work themselves, but the facilitator's knowledge of the broader context will often enable him or her to link workers with other people who are sympathetic to their activities or who can provide important information or other resources. Linking participants to a supportive network provides them not only with emotional support but often with organizational and community support.

The linking of participants in networks of support sometimes enables them to engage new people in research activities and extends the breadth and power of the research process itself. When people display interest, it may be appropriate to ask them if they would like to participate in activities or to help the research workers perform their tasks. In this way, linking not only extends the support network for individual participants but generates the energy that sustains a community-building process.

As research facilitators assist other participants in developing supportive links, they should be wary of inserting themselves as permanent intermediaries in the linking process. When they continue to act as "middlemen," research facilitators inhibit the development of positive working relationships between participants and others with whom they work. They maintain control and increase their own power in the situation at the expense of those they are assisting. Figure 6.2. depicts a situation in which information transfer, discussion, or interaction cannot take place except through the research facilitator. A linking, suppor-

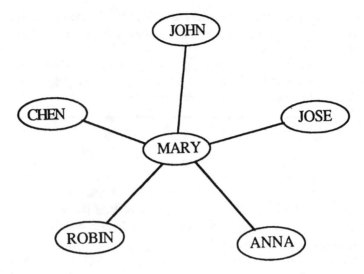

Figure 6.2. A Controlled Network

tive network, on the other hand, provides multiple opportunities for exchange, conversation, and consultation (see Figure 6.3).

Reviewing

Participants should meet on a regular basis to review their progress. At these meetings, the plan should be displayed, and stakeholders and each of the participants performing tasks should be given the opportunity to do the following:

- Review the plan. (Focus question: Have you had any thoughts on our plan?)
- Report on progress. (How are you going with your tasks?)
- Modify sections of the plan, if necessary. (Are you having any difficulties? Do we need to change our approach? Do we need to change the tasks you've been assigned?)
- Celebrate successes. (What have we achieved?)

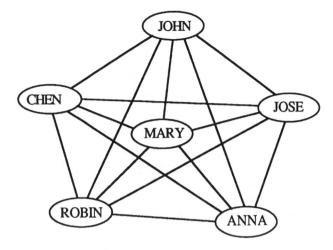

Figure 6.3. A Linking Network

These activities motivate people by highlighting accomplishments or reassuring them if they have failed to make significant progress; in addition, they provide a context that reinforces their sense of community. As people strive to perform their tasks and report on their successes and struggles, they share their worlds in a real, direct way and, in the process, extend their understanding of the contexts in which they are working.

These processes also present opportunities for rethinking aspects of the description, interpretation, and planning processes and provide extra support for people experiencing difficulty. Participants may find, for instance, that they require more information, that the tasks they have been set turn out to be inappropriate in some way, or that their activities are being blocked. In these cases, the plan will need to be modified to take these exigencies into account.

The reiterative nature of action research soon becomes apparent. Where people struggle to implement activities derived from a fixed vision or version of their world, they will soon be confronted by the dynamic realities of the context. To the extent that they can construct and reconstruct their vision, taking into account the increased understanding that comes from each reiteration of the process, so they will successfully negotiate the complex web of meanings, interactions, and discourses that compose social life.

Evaluating

At some stage, the need for a formal evaluation of the project may become evident. People who contributed funds and personal or political support will probably appreciate some statement or report that provides information about the extent to which progress has been made or desired ends have been achieved.

Evaluation requires processes that are similar in nature to those used to formulate joint stakeholder descriptions and interpretations. A full treatment of the process is provided in Guba and Lincoln's *Fourth Generation Evaluation* (1989). Evaluation is carried out as a joint construction of stakeholder groups who do the following:

- Place their claims, concerns, and issues on the table for consideration.
- Review information obtained from interviews, observation, documents, and group constructions.
- Resolve claims, issues, and concerns.
- Prioritize unresolved items.

Through a process of description and reflection, those tasks and activities that have led to a satisfactory resolution are delineated, and those that are unresolved become subject to negotiation concerning continued action. As Guba and Lincoln (1989) point out, different values held by different stakeholders will lead to disagreement about priorities for further action. The research facilitator's task is to negotiate these points of disagreement and seek ways to reformulate the issues so that participants can agree on the next steps to be taken.

This method of evaluation is consonant with the constructivist philosophy that is inherent in community-based action research. It defines outcomes in ends that are acceptable to stakeholders, rather than those whose degree of success may be measured against some set of fixed criteria.

Sometimes, there is considerable pressure to provide a "definitive" evaluation, especially from people who wish to use numbers to justify expenditure or their personal involvement. Numbers, however, are illusory and usually reflect a distorted vision of the research process. Nevertheless, there are occasions when some quantitative information is useful and may be properly included in an evaluation process. We may provide numbers of students enrolled in a course, youth attending a program, mothers attending a child care clinic, and so on. Numbers by themselves are misleading, however, and often oversimplify the state of affairs. They also risk reifying—creating an illusory preeminence about—certain aspects of a project or program. People may focus on tables that quantify relatively trivial features or disregard significant features of the project. Research participants should be wary, therefore, of engaging in forms of evaluation that are contrary to the principles of community-based action research. (A number of appropriate evaluation strategies are summarized by Yolanda Wadsworth in her book *Everyday Evaluation on the Run,* 1997.)

Conclusion

As I was writing this chapter, I described it to friends as "the sharp end of the stick." It is the point at which action occurs—where we set out actually to do something about the problems that have been the driving force behind all the activity. I have described routines that suggest ways to work with stakeholders to plan tasks and activities, implement them, sustain them, and evaluate them. The end point of the process should be the resolution of the problems with which we started.

Social life is rarely as simple as that, however. We usually find that myriad issues emerge when we start to poke at a problem, which can transform the problem itself and our orientation toward it. Steps taken to solve one problem sometimes take the lid off a whole range of related issues and problems. Further, the broader the context in which a problem is held, and the greater the number of stakeholders, the greater the complexity of the task confronting researchers. Chapter 7 focuses on these more complex situations and provides guidance to researchers who wish to engage deep-seated problems within relatively diverse social, organizational, and community settings.

BOX 6.1
Act: Resolving Problems

PURPOSE:

To formulate practical solutions to problems that have been the focus
of research

PROCESS:

Plan

Priorities: Arrange projected actions in order of importance
Goals: State the broad actions required to resolve prioritized
issues
Objectives: List actions required to accomplish goal(s)
Tasks: Stipulate the sequence of tasks required to accomplish
each action
Persons: Specify those who will carry out the tasks
Time: Determine time frame within which each task will be
completed
Resources: Calculate materials, equipment, and funds required to
complete tasks

Implement

Communicate: Inform people of each other's activities
Nurture: Praise people's efforts
Reflect: Assist participants in reflecting on problems and
progress
Assist: Actively assist people when difficulties hinder progress
Model: Apply working principles in all activities
Link: Connect people in a mutually supportive network

Evaluate

Review the plan
Assess the effect of activities
Revise the plan if needed
Prioritize unresolved issues
Celebrate achievements

Act

RESOLVING COMPLEX PROBLEMS

Chapter 6 provided routines for moving a simple research process from the interpretive or analytic stage to practical action within limited contexts such as classrooms, offices, and small organizations. This chapter will focus on more complicated contexts, in which practitioners engage the complex issues and deep-seated problems often contained within large and diverse organizations, such as government agencies and business corporations, and/or that cover multiple community or organizational contexts in cities, regions, and states.

A full treatment of the organization and management of large-scale projects and programs is beyond the scope of this book, but in this chapter I will present procedures that can help participants enact a relatively complex community-based action research process. These procedures are also relevant to research facilitators whose small action research processes have grown exponentially to encompass increasingly complex problems, issues, and contexts.

In the mid-1980s, I worked as a member of a small team of Aboriginal and non-Aboriginal people to develop the Centre for Aboriginal Studies in our university. Using an existing program as an organizational base, we obtained funding that enabled us to investigate the training needs of Aboriginal people in Western Australia. Through time, we built a detailed picture of the needs of Aboriginal people, not only in relation to training but in relation to their broader social, cultural, and community lives.

Initially, short courses and workshops presented to local groups met some of their immediate, short-term needs. It soon became apparent, however, that the complex, long-term needs of Aboriginal people could not be met by ad hoc, short-term training programs. In the following years, we developed a number of long-term courses, programs, and services that focused on issues that were of high priority for Aboriginal people in a wide range of contexts. These courses included management, community development, health, addiction, and culturally appropriate work practices.

In subsequent years, we planned and implemented a wide range of programs and services that required increasingly complex activity as we integrated the needs of culturally diverse client groups with the bureaucratic demands of a large university. The group of 5 or 6 people who commenced with a small budget in 1984 grew within a few years to a staff in excess of 60 and a multimillion-dollar budget.

The potential to provide programs and services to people across the state and to institute positive social change for Aboriginal people increased dramatically. As the operation grew, however, we had to extend our knowledge and skills to enable those developments to take place. We learned about organizational development, community development, management, budgeting, planning, curriculum development, micropolitics, negotiating, training, and many other things. We also learned to recognize our own limitations as we realized the extent to which we were dependent on the input and goodwill of the community.

Although the basic "look, think, act" framework remains the same for more complex projects, practitioners need to modify and adapt their procedures and acquire additional skills to enable them to accomplish the multiple intents of community-based action research. This chapter therefore focuses on planning and organizational arrangements that will help participants maintain control and direction of their activities in these more demanding circumstances. The following sections describe appropriate orientations to management, long-term planning processes, organizational arrangements for implementing activities, evaluation procedures, and the value of celebration.

Managing Community-Based Action Research

As an integral part of a complex social system, researchers always affect other people's lives in some way when they modify their work practices or initiate new activities. Researchers are likely to disrupt practices that have long been institutionalized and that can have impacts on people's egos, dignity, power, status, and career opportunities. In almost all situations, some people will resist changes of any sort unless the processes are carefully defined and their interests taken into account.

Significant change is also likely to connect with many agencies and organizations, so that participants may find themselves subject to pressures to develop controlling and bureaucratic styles of operation that lose their community focus and override the principles of community-based action research. Facilitators must work with participants to ensure that they are able to maintain the autonomy and integrity of their work but avoid the style, manner, and forms of operation that typify many bureaucratic settings. They need, above all, to maintain approaches to their work that preserve active participation and a sense of community among all participants.

The unit for which I once worked was asked to produce a program to provide management training for people in community agencies. We estimated that development processes would take a minimum of 6 months and resisted efforts to get us to contract to do the job in 6 weeks, a period that would have allowed no time for consultation with client groups. The contract was given to another organization, which developed a set of training programs within the 6 weeks allotted. After 6 months of ineffectual activity, however, the training programs folded. We eventually acquired funding for a 12-month developmental process, which resulted in a program that is still operating successfully today across all regions of the state.

In another instance, we estimated that we would need 6 months to consult local groups and formulate a redevelopment strategy for a regional community organization. Although we were funded, after negotiation, for only 4 months, we found ways of completing the job satisfactorily in that time. Today, 5 years later, that regional organization is still operating effectively.

To integrate their activities with existing organizations and agencies, participants should constantly refer to the working principles of community-based action research. They need to inform themselves of approaches to management that are consonant with those principles so that they can enact their organizing activities in appropriate ways. Books such as Block's *The Empowered Manager* (1990) and Peck's *A World Waiting to Be Born* (1993) are examples of literature that provide such orientations.

Block (1990) suggests a way of conceptualizing the difference between what he typifies as *bureaucratic* and *entrepreneurial* organizations. Bureaucratic organizations, he suggests, are characterized by patriarchal systems that emphasize a top-down, high-control orientation to organizational activity. These types of organizations breed power-oriented people who use manipulative tactics to further their myopic self-interests, which focus on advancement, approval by organizational superiors, money, safety, and increased control, rather than on service. Block further suggests that one outcome of this style of operation is the creation of cautious, dependent people who work in ways that maintain what they have.

A sign in bold capital letters on the wall of an alternative school program proclaimed, "IF YOU KEEP DOING WHAT YOU ALWAYS DO, YOU'LL KEEPING GETTING WHAT YOU ALWAYS GET."

Entrepreneurial organizations, on the other hand, are characterized, according to Block, by people who act out of "enlightened self-interest." Enlightened self-interest focuses on activities that have meaning, depth, and substance; that genuinely serve the interests of clients or users; that have integrity; and that have positive impacts on people's lives. Entrepreneurial organizations are based on trust and a belief in the responsibility of people. The business of such organizations is managed directly and authentically, so that people know where they stand, share information, share control, and are willing to take reasonable risks. Supervision, in these circumstances, becomes oriented toward support and consultation rather than control, and success is defined as contribution and service to service users, clients, or customers.

Although Block's conceptual frameworks have a business orientation, his entrepreneurial approach to management emphasizes a service-oriented definition of self-interest that is in harmony with the principles of community-based action research. He proposes that management is not necessarily as highly controlling and exploitative as is sometimes perceived but can be enacted in consonance with more humanistic and democratic forms of organizational life.

As community-based research projects increase in extent and complexity, the tools and resources of management become increasingly relevant. Research facilitators and other participants need organizational and management skills to manage the wide range of activities, constraints, forces, and pressures that impinge on their activities. They also need, however, to be consciously aware of the model of management they are enacting so that they are not drawn into procedures based on traditional, hierarchical models of authority and control that damage, rather than enhance, community-based research processes.

Planning

Difficult problems and complex settings often require long-term and large-scale preparation, sometimes called *strategic planning*. Strategic planning encompasses carefully defined and inclusive procedures that provide participants with a clear vision of their directions and intentions. It enables stakeholders to describe

- A *vision* of their long-term aspirations
- An *operational plan* that defines the particular projects or activities that will accomplish this vision
- *Action* plans that lay out the tasks and steps required to enact each of these projects or activities

A Unifying Vision

As people work toward a collective vision that clarifies the nature of the problems that have brought them together, they gain a greater understanding of the complexities of the situation in which they are enmeshed. They also gain a more holistic understanding of the multitude of factors within which problems are embedded and realize the need to formulate increasingly sophisticated plans to resolve them.

The use of drugs by youth, for instance, may encompass a whole range of factors, including education, family, lifestyle, work, leisure activities, and the media. A community seriously intent on dealing with the issue of drug abuse will need to take all these factors into account in planning. Although community members need to focus on activities that will have immediate impacts on some aspects of the problem, they also need to do "upstream" work that goes to its sources, rather than deal only superficially with its manifestations.

The story goes that a man rescued a number of people from drowning in a river. Eventually, he tired of dragging one after the other from the river and walked upstream, where he observed a bully pushing people into the water. He struggled with the bully, who was eventually arrested and taken away. The problem of the drowning people was solved by his "upstream" work.

When we engage in action research, we are often placed in situations where we need to be pulling people from the water and working upstream at the same time. It is important, however, that we go to the source of the problem, rather than do nothing but cope constantly with its outcomes.

As their analysis reveals the factors with which they must contend, stakeholders may be able to rationalize their activities. By planning carefully, they may find that they are able to incorporate a diversity of activities into a few broad schemes or to connect a multitude of activities in ways that increase their effectiveness. A vision of the future that encompasses many facets of their common life may start to emerge.

A vision statement should clearly define the long-term aspirations of the stakeholders. It should attempt to articulate the ultimate ends of an action research project by encompassing statements about particular goals within a broader framework of ideas. Such a statement may take the following form:

> Students, administrators, and teachers at Downerton School will work with parents and other relevant community groups to provide a high quality of education for families in the district. They will develop a curriculum and a school organization that is relevant to the lives of students and enables them to
>
> - Achieve the highest levels of academic success of which they are capable
> - Gain and maintain high levels of self-fulfillment
> - Develop and enact moral and ethical standards appropriate to their family and community lives
> - Live in harmony with fellow students, staff, and the community at large
> - Gain the skills and knowledge that will enable them to be a viable part of the workforce

The development of a vision is an attempt to integrate the many agendas that emerge from analyses in the "think" phase of community-based action research.

The vision statement should provide the rubric under which the concerns of all participants are incorporated—academic standards, student behavior, boring teaching, irrelevant curriculum, teen pregnancy, and so on. Although different participants—teachers, administrators, students, and parents—might have different agendas and priorities, they should all identify with and accept ownership of a vision statement within which they can recognize their own agendas and interests.

Vision statements should be publicly developed as part of the community-based planning processes outlined in Chapter 6. The above statement would result not solely from the activities of school administration, faculty, and/or school board, for instance, but from an extended process including all stakeholders—students, parents, community groups, business interests, and so on.

Vision statements are not the beginning point of an action research process. They arise only after considerable work has been undertaken to define specific problems and result from efforts to rationalize a variety of issues and concerns that have emanated from initial research processes. The "big plan" is an emergent reality, rather than a predefined and predefining one.

Operational Statements: Enacting the Vision

An operational statement delineates the specific projects that enable participants to realize their vision. The above vision statement, for instance, may be operationalized as follows:

The Downerton School will enact its vision through

- A community-based curriculum development process
- Site-based management processes
- Parent participation projects, including classroom volunteers, fund-raising, after-school programs, and short-term specific-needs projects
- A student governance organization

- Peer counseling program
- Community outreach and education programs
- Staff development programs

The intended actions stated here are based on what the various primary participants view as necessary to help them deal with their issues and concerns. Students cannot demand that their teachers engage in staff development programs; teachers cannot initiate sex education programs for the students. Actions must derive from the people who are the targets of any suggested action. The teachers themselves will be unresponsive to staff development programs that have been mandated for them, and students are likely to see a sex education program as yet another imposition of the adult world unless it results from their own analysis of their needs.

I once observed a group of practitioners planning a program to decrease teenage alcohol consumption in one community. Their basic premise was, "How can we stop them from drinking?" The only involvement of teenagers envisaged was to use some "respectable" teens as leaders to act as models. There was no thought of involving teenagers who actually consumed alcohol. I do not know the actual outcome of the program, but I would be surprised if the group's efforts resulted in a decrease in alcohol consumption.

There is sometimes a tendency to "gang up" on a problem by eliciting the support of many individuals and agencies. Plans to solve youth problems in a community sometimes start with meetings of concerned citizens or community leaders, who then seek the aid of social workers, teachers, other community leaders, service organizations, churches, government agencies, and politicians to develop appropriate plans. Although any or all of these may be appropriate at some stage, community-based action research emphasizes the primacy of the principal stakeholders—those whose interests are centrally at stake.

Action essentially must derive, in this case, from the youth themselves, who must ultimately formulate plans and decide what and who will be involved in the solutions they define.

Operational statements should be comprehensive and should describe the activities required to enable the primary stakeholders to accomplish the aspects of the vision that are significant to them. Participants may not be able or willing to institute all the activities at once, but the operational statement should clearly articulate all the factors that need to be taken into account to resolve the problem effectively. Research facilitators should arrange meetings that enable participants to review their vision and operational statements from time to time so that they are aware of the extent to which they have made progress toward solution of their problems. An operational statement diminishes the possibility that people will look to "one-shot jobs" as instant solutions that focus on one related element.

▧ Action Plans

A separate plan should be developed for each of the activities or projects delineated in the operational statement. As each plan becomes activated, participants should define the following:

- The *objectives* of the project
- The *tasks* to be done
- The *steps* to be taken for each task
- The *people* involved
- The *places* where activity will occur
- The *timelines* and durations of activities
- The *resources* required

Processes for developing action plans are described more fully in Chapter 6.

As different teams or committees formulate their action plans, it is important that they come together to reveal their activities and directions to each other. This provides opportunities for the various smaller groups to rationalize and coordinate activities, so that plans do not work at cross-purposes or waste resources by inadvertently engaging in activities in the same areas.

Reviewing the Plans

As participants prepare to implement activities, they should appraise the strength of each plan according to the internal and external forces that impinge on it. A simple framework involving an analysis of the internal strengths and weaknesses of the plan, and external opportunities and threats, guides this process.

Strengths and Weaknesses, Opportunities and Threats

- *Strengths:* What are the strengths of the group (e.g., people and purposes)? What are the strengths of the plan (e.g., processes, resources, funds, materials, and places)?
- *Weaknesses:* What are the weaknesses of the group? Of the plan? Who is not included? What resources are unavailable? What skills or knowledge do we need to obtain? Are there any gaps in our planning?
- *Opportunities:* What can we do that we have not yet planned to do? Have we taken full advantage of the people and resources we have? Who might potentially assist us? What resources are available that we are not yet using?
- *Threats:* Who might resist our efforts? What might they do? Are we invading other people's territory? Who might perceive us as a threat?

As answers to these and other relevant questions emerge, they should be reformulated in the form of objectives or tasks and assigned to individuals or groups as part of their responsibilities. For instance, a weakness identified as "inadequate funds" should be restated as an objective: "to investigate possible sources of funding" or "to commence the following fund-raising activities." People can be assigned these tasks as part of the project.

▨ Political Dimensions

In the 1960s, action research was often enacted through campaigns in which groups achieved their objectives by engaging in overtly social and political action. Community-based action research is not oriented toward this social action approach. Its purposes and objectives are to formulate links with and among parties who might be seen to be in conflict and to negotiate settlements of interest that allow all stakeholders to enhance their group life. To the extent that research facilitators are able to do this, they will increase the potential for the common unity that is at the heart of this approach to research. When researchers engage in political processes based on polarities of interest, they are likely to engage in conflictual interactions that generate antagonism. Although the potential for short-term gains is enticing, long-term enmities, in my experience, have a habit of coming back to bite you. The first impulse in community-based action research must be to build links and formulate complementary coalitions, rather than to divide the social setting into friends and enemies.

During my work with Aboriginal people, I have become increasingly sensitive to the tendency of some individuals constantly to cast Aboriginals as "oppressed" peoples who are "victims" of colonization. To define Aboriginal life in such terms is to build a vision that has the potential to demean and diminish a group whose cultural strength and spiritual wisdom have significance that goes far beyond their small numbers. To portray them in such terms is, from my perspective, an act of envictimization.

This does not mean that I wish to deny the exceedingly violent history that has been visited on Aboriginal people in Australia, or to diminish the social, cultural, and political problems they face. There are times when we need to confront those issues directly and forcefully. When I consider the strength and integrity of my Aboriginal colleagues and friends and the vitality of their family lives, however, I see a broader reality that goes far beyond this vision of Aboriginal-as-victim. I don't want to diminish their human potential by constantly highlighting their oppression or portraying them as victims. The words that my Aboriginal colleagues use to speak of their experience provide a vision of familial, cultural, and spiritual strength that is a much more powerful basis for action. I would rather build from that strength than struggle through weakness.

There may be times when obdurate, inflexible, ambitious, or fearful people will try to block the progress of a project. Research facilitators need to be aware of the political dimensions of the settings in which they work to deal with these situations. They can list those individuals and groups who are likely to assist them or to be in favor of their activities, as well as those who are likely to resist because they believe the researchers' activities to be against their interests. All these people should be included as stakeholders from the beginning of the research process.

Only when researchers have failed, despite their best attempts, to engage people in their projects, and when people have purposively set themselves against the researchers' aims, should researchers fall back on the strategies envisaged in such books as Coover, Deacon, Esser, and Moore's *Resource Manual for a Living Revolution* (1985) or engage in the "campaigning" mode suggested by Kelly and Sewell in *With Head, Heart, and Hand* (1988).

Financial Planning

Funding sometimes can be a contentious and awkward aspect of a project, and research facilitators need to handle finances carefully and openly to maintain the integrity of the research process. Facilitators should assist participants in formulating a clearly defined budget that links financial requirements to each of the tasks and activities defined in the original planning process. The budget must be set out clearly, so that it can be understood by all stakeholders. They should be presented with a copy of the budget, prior to meetings if possible, and have the opportunity to discuss it during meetings.

The budget should estimate the costs involved in establishing a project as well as continuing (recurrent) costs. These may be set out as

TABLE 7.1 Sample Budget Table for Youth Leisure Project

	Task 1	Task 2	Task 3	Task 4	Task 5
Salaries and consultants					
Materials and equipment					
Travel					
Telephone					
Total					

shown in Table 7.1, which is based on a budget table used in a youth leisure project.

An extended project that involves complex processes may require the services of someone with budgeting expertise, but participants can learn to formulate budgets for less complex projects. It is important that all costs be itemized and that decisions be made about expenditures— whether, for instance, people are to be hired for some tasks, what equipment is required, and what travel is necessary.

Finances are often the most contentious part of a community-based process because of most people's experiences with bureaucratic organizational settings, where power and authority are invested in those delegated to control the finances. When decisions must be made about funding priorities, they should be made at meetings of stakeholders. In working through these controversial issues and the negotiation of sometimes conflicting demands, a group can establish feelings of purpose and unity. When people in positions of power make forced decisions, divisions and antagonism often result.

My high school history teacher constantly emphasized, "He who holds the purse strings holds the power!" Researchers should keep this in mind when pursuing empowering, community-based processes.

Decisions must also be made about where funds are to be held. Public finances are usually held within some incorporated body (e.g., the Gleneagle Youth Association) that has the facility to dispense and account for monies. The problem here is that the incorporated body itself has restrictions placed on the ways in which monies can be spent, with implications for the project. As a project increases in size, the group responsible for initiating activities may need to be formally incorporated to acquire and disburse funds. These are contingencies that project facilitators should take into account as they lead people through a research process.

People sometimes are tempted to develop projects or programs because grant monies are available. They either launch into projects that are only peripherally relevant to their purposes or find themselves striving valiantly to fulfill the conflicting demands of the grant and the research project. In the process, the focus of their activities moves away from the issues and concerns that provide the energy for the formation of community, and participants risk burnout, disillusionment, or loss of direction.

Participants in community-based action research projects should formulate specific plans to ensure that they have adequate funding for the period of the project. In many instances, people set up programs, services, or facilities with seed grants (grants that are given one time only, for specific purposes) only to find that they have no continuing funding. On the other hand, however, people should not restrict themselves to action for which funding is available. Research facilitators need to do a delicate dance to enable participants to actualize their dreams through their own efforts without leading them into situations of failure.

A good friend of mine used to view government funding with suspicion. "Stay away from government funding," he would say. "You'll kill yourself. Do what you can with your own resources."

Certainly, the situation of the Aboriginal community school I described in Chapter 1 is testimony to this counsel. The teacher who assisted the community in its formation admitted to me in conversation that she doubts whether the school would have been so successful if the people hadn't had to struggle to get it going.

Implementing:
Researchers Organizing Themselves

When action research projects expand to encompass increasingly large numbers of groups and projects, research facilitators need to manage affairs efficiently to minimize duplication, to keep track of the way resources are being used, and to keep themselves on course. Many forces are likely to intervene as research projects become increasingly large and successful. Individuals or groups may try to appropriate the projects or the resources they contain for their own benefit, or projects may become so large and unwieldy that parts of them drift off to pursue other courses.

The task of research facilitators is to organize activities so that the momentum of the project continues to build and the research process continues to function productively. The activities of the project must be coherent and must remain directed to stakeholders' problems and issues, or enthusiasm and participation are likely to fade. Research facilitators should help participants make organizational arrangements that will maintain the coherence and sense of purpose of the research process as it progresses. They will need to consider the following:

- An organizational base
- Organizational arrangements
- Guiding the research process, by using appropriate
  Operational principles
  Language
  Decision-making processes
  Support and monitoring processes

An Organizational Base

Although relatively simple projects may be organized by informal groups or committees, more complex projects will require more formal organizational arrangements. This will become particularly evident as research processes begin to connect with the operations of public institutions, agencies, business corporations, or community organizations.

When significant levels of funding are acquired, projects will need to become affiliated with existing formal organizations or take steps to become formally incorporated bodies. In the latter case, all stakeholders should be thoroughly informed of the procedures involved in setting up such bodies and should participate in formulating policies and procedures.

Sometimes, it is easier to set up a committee within an existing institution or organization. The research facilitator should be wary of taking this step, however, because research processes are easily taken over or distorted by the policies and procedures of established organizations. Further, existing institutions, agencies, and organizations are sometimes held in disfavor by, or are alienated from, some stakeholder groups, to the extent that they may be unwilling to work under the auspices of particular organizations. Members of marginalized groups, for instance, are particularly distrustful of government agencies and institutions, often perceiving them as agents of control as much as service deliverers.

Research facilitators, therefore, should assist participants in exploring the potentials and threats involved in organizing their activities under the auspices of any existing organizations. If they decide to do so, they should put organizational procedures and practices into place that will ensure the autonomy of the research group.

For a number of years now, I have been aware of the strength of the Centre for Aboriginal Studies, for which I work. As part of a large university, it has been able to use that institution's significant resources to develop innovative and powerful programs and services for Aboriginal people. Still, this strength has not been accomplished without many battles along the way, as Centre staff have struggled to ensure that their work is "Aboriginalized"—that is, that it maintains Aboriginal people at the center of organizational life and provides services and programs that are socially and culturally appropriate to Aboriginal people.

The Centre blunts the force of university policies and procedures in two ways. First, the Centre has a policy statement that clearly defines "Aboriginalization" and "Aboriginal Terms of Reference" as central tenets of its policies. Second, it has an Aboriginal Advisory Committee, which is the policy-making body of the Centre and the final arbiter in disputes relating to its policies and functions. Third, as part of the policy of Aboriginalization, all senior leadership positions in the Centre are held by Aboriginal people. Organizational arrangements, therefore, work to maintain the autonomy of the Centre and the authenticity of its work within the university setting.

When it is clear that an independent organization is required, research facilitators will need to familiarize themselves with procedures for incorporation. The organization will need clearly established purposes, an organizational structure, operating procedures, and arrangements for accounting for funds.

Organizational Arrangements

The bureaucratic style inherent in most modern organizations emphasizes hierarchies of control and systems of subordination and dominance that often are in conflict with the principles of community-based action research. Organizational diagrams are often represented as hierarchies, or systems of superiority and subordination, with the most senior or most powerful person at the top (see Figure 7.1).

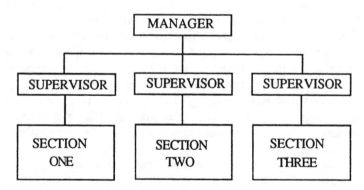

Figure 7.1. A Hierarchical Organization

When researchers organize for community-based action research, they need to ensure how the relationships of authority common in bureaucratic forms of organization are inscribed in their own work. Care taken with language will assist in this process. It is best to think of *teams, clusters,* or *groups* rather than *departments* or *divisions* (note the images those words evoke). It is better to have *representatives* or *coordinators* than *directors, supervisors,* or *heads.* Both researchers' behavior and the symbolic universe within which it is encompassed should enhance the empowering intent of the research activities.

If participants in a research process need to depict an organizational hierarchy because they are working within an existing bureaucracy, they can reframe the hierarchy by turning the organizational chart upside down and changing the terminology (see Figure 7.2). For a more graphic representation of a community-based organization, the coordinators can be nested with the team members (Figure 7.3). It is also possible to list the teams vertically, with the facilitator over to the side, or to draw the teams in a circle. However they are drawn, graphic organizational representations should reflect the intent of equality and unity rather than superiority, subordination, and division, and coordination and support rather than control and supervision. They should embody the organizational and operational intent of community-based action research.

In keeping with this dictum, teams should be self-managing, so that members are responsible for scheduling their own meetings and organizing activities, assigning jobs, purchasing materials, recruiting other

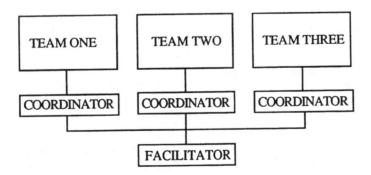

Figure 7.2. A Reversed Hierarchy

Figure 7.3. A Community-Based Organization
NOTE: O = team member; X = coordinator.

workers, and so on. All decisions related to the attainment of a team's objectives should be made by team members, although any significant change in direction or purpose should be referred to a meeting of all stakeholders for discussion and endorsement.

Coordinators may also meet to integrate the activities of each group so that activities do not overlap or come into conflict. Research facilitators should encourage teams to meet regularly so that people can review their activities, share ideas, strengthen relationships, and, in the process, reinforce their sense of community.

This extended discussion of organizational charts may seem to be somewhat trivial and out of place in an introductory handbook, but it serves as a reminder that the system of signs and symbols embedded in our language and our graphics has a subtle, pervasive, and powerful influence on the way we perceive others and interact with them.

Guiding the Research Process

Principles in Operation

The literature of management is replete with concepts such as *supervision, leadership,* and *control,* which are antithetical to the principles of community-based research. Hierarchical styles of management embody processes that engage centralized decision making, in which people in superior positions define courses of action to be taken, and relationships of dominance and subordination, in which obedience to authority is assumed to provide the best way to get things done.

Management of a community-based process, however, requires a different approach to operation and organization. As facilitators assist participants in organizing and implementing activities, they should consciously enact the key concepts and principles of community-based research, constantly providing participants with information about what is happening, maintaining positive working relationships, and including all stakeholders as active participants in planning and decision-making activities.

Meeting times, places, and agendas should be known to *all* participants, and procedures for dealing with people's issues or concerns should be clearly articulated. Coordinators should have clearly defined procedures for passing on the outcomes of coordination meetings to their team members, and all stakeholders should be regularly informed about activities and events. All participants should be able to take advantage of opportunities to engage other stakeholders in activities and events related to the processes of inquiry.

Using Appropriate Language

When talking with others, people provide not only direct information but also many subtle, powerful messages that signify an orientation to the listener. The way we speak and the words we use carry implicit messages about the relative status and worth of the speaker and listener and the nature of their interaction. In general terms, therefore, it is better for research facilitators to use inclusive forms of language that have a connotation of togetherness—the first-person plural *we* rather than the first-person singular *I* or the third-person *you* or *they*. Facilitators who ask, "How do you want to do this?" subtly alienate themselves from the process. "How can we do this?" is a more inclusive form of the same question that implies that the facilitator is an equal member of the team.

Examine the following questions and statements for the implicit messages embedded in them:

- How can we make kids stop wearing that sort of clothing?
- How can we get parents to become more involved in the school?
- I think that you need to develop an antismoking campaign.
- I don't like the way you've done this.

Each of these implies relationships of control, authority, and exclusion that are all the more powerful because we usually accept the form of the message as we concentrate on its content. Language orients us to our world and to each other; appropriate language thus becomes a fundamental cornerstone of community-based action research.

Making Decisions

Significant decisions about policies, purposes, objectives, tasks, organizational structure, general procedures, and the allocation of funds and resources should be made at meetings attended by all stakeholders or their spokespersons. All stakeholders should know what is happening and have the opportunity to contribute to discussions about issues. This process sometimes can be tedious as stakeholders are brought up to speed on the organizational limitations within which many of their activities are bounded. Equality of worth, however, is bound up with equality of knowledge. If parents, clients, and other community members do not understand the circumstances in which they are working, they are not in a position to become fully active participants in the research process.

This approach may seem a time-consuming and sometimes inefficient way to go about to decision making, but the investment can pay off bountifully in the long run. People who are clearly informed about purposes and procedures are likely to invest themselves energetically in activities and to work tenaciously to maintain their ownership of the research process. Decisions made by an inner circle of experts, administrators, or "loaded" committees, on the other hand, are apt to be viewed with suspicion and to achieve only low levels of support.

I once attended a meeting at which 3 days of intensive work were required to articulate a plan for a regional organization that had become so inefficient it could no longer operate effectively. Representatives from the different stakeholding groups in the region attended this meeting and worked through the issues meticulously and deliberately.

Because extensive preparatory work had been conducted with all stakeholding groups, there was considerable agreement on most issues. Nevertheless, many details had to be worked through carefully to ensure that the functions and operations of the regional body did not interfere with the work of local groups. At each stage of the proceedings, time was allocated to allow participants, as individuals or as representatives of their groups, to voice concerns or bring forward issues that needed to be addressed.

After 3 days, consensus was reached about the basic constitution of the regional body, and interim officeholders who would initiate the new body were elected. Six years later, that organization is still operating effectively, although it deals with contentious matters among groups of people who are often in conflict. The time taken to work through the issues with all stakeholders has been repaid many times over.

Research facilitators and other participants should make decisions by consensus, following procedures that ensure that everyone is clear on what is planned and how it will work. Resolutions made on the basis of a vote often leave the agendas of marginal groups neglected and sap the energy of a community. Although major decisions about policy, purpose, and objectives are made corporately by stakeholders, detailed planning of tasks and activities should be left to the people responsible for carrying them out. This provides a sense of responsibility, competence, and autonomy that heightens people's feelings of ownership of the research process.

Support and Monitoring

In Chapter 6, I emphasized the need to provide participants with support as they enact their action plans. This is an important function for facilitators or team coordinators, whose task is to assist participants in marshaling their energies, monitoring their activities, and maintaining a focus on their purposes. Facilitators and team coordinators should talk regularly with project members, giving them opportunities to reflect on their activities and providing feedback. Their role is not to supervise, evaluate, or judge participants' performance but to act as consultants, providing information, advice, or assistance to team members. The demeanor and behavior of facilitators and coordinators always should imply that they are resource or support persons, rather than bosses or organizational superiors.

Evaluating

As stakeholders work through the recursive processes of observation, reflection, planning, and review, they are involved in a constant process of evaluation that enables them to monitor their activities and their progress. There may be times, however, when a formal review of a project or program is either required by a funding agency or perceived as necessary to the project. When people take the time to stand back from their day-to-day activities to explore and reflect on the processes in which they have been engaged and to share perceptions and interpretations, they gain greater clarity about the direction of their work and efficacy of their activities.

Evaluation needs to be clearly focused to achieve its desired purposes. If evaluation includes a mass of detail that is only peripherally relevant and fails to capture the crucial elements at the core of the project, then it may be counterproductive, directing attention to the wrong areas of activity and distorting the research process.

Steps to Evaluation

Purpose:
Who Will Benefit From the Project?

Evaluation should, ultimately, assess the worth of a set of activities or a project according to its impacts on the primary stakeholders. Many evaluations focus on the activities in which project members engage but fail to provide any indication of the extent to which the process has made an impact on the lives of the people for whom the project was formulated.

I once helped a group of community workers in reviewing a program that engaged them in a diverse array of activities with many community groups. They enjoyed the work they were doing and were busy, and their efforts appeared to be appreciated by the people with whom they worked. Such was the extent of their activities that some of them were feeling stressed and overworked.

When I asked the community workers to estimate the extent to which their activities contributed to the purposes of the program—an increase in work opportunities for unemployed youth—they were silent. Although they had engaged in many activities with youth in the community, none could make any connection between the activities in which they were engaged and the specific purposes of their program. Young people, it seemed, did not have increased work opportunities as a result of their enterprise.

Audience:
Who Will Read the Evaluation Report?

Prior to commencing an evaluation, the research facilitator should define the groups to whom the results of the evaluation will be reported. The processes and products will differ depending on the audiences. Is the evaluation being conducted for those who provide funds, those who control the organization, those who are the recipients of services, those for whom the project was initiated, those who provide the services, or any other stakeholder group? Answers to these questions will help the facilitator formulate a suitable evaluation process and present the resulting report in an appropriate form.

Procedures:
How Is the Evaluation Carried Out?

Evaluation is an intrinsic part of the action research cycle. The period of evaluation is a time when researchers formally examine or review the processes in which they have been engaged—another cycle in the "look, think, act" process. In evaluation, the processes are as follows:

- *Look:* Describe all that the participants have been doing.
- *Think:* Reflect on what the participants have been doing. Note areas of success and any deficiencies, issues, or problems.
- *Act:* Judge the worth, effectiveness, appropriateness, and outcomes of those activities.

In keeping with the principles of community-based action research, however, evaluation is not carried out by an outside evaluator to make judgments about the worth, effectiveness, success, or failure of a project. It is a process that enables those who have been engaged in the research project to learn from their own experience. In Chapter 6, I provided some detail on the constructivist approach to evaluation advocated by Guba and Lincoln (1989), an orientation to evaluation that is in harmony with the philosophical principles of community-based action research. Another example is provided by Wadsworth's *Everyday Evaluation on the Run* (1997).

In some instances, agencies that provide funding will require a more directive form of evaluation to assess the extent to which project activities have attained their purposes or objectives. In this case, evaluation moves through a more direct cycle of activities. It requires participants to do the following:

- Define the purposes and audiences of the evaluation.
- Determine the goals of the project (What is the purpose? What is to be achieved? For whom? What are the intended outcomes and for whom? e.g., "to increase the rate of employment of youth in Queenstown").
- Set the objectives (What will be done to achieve the purposes; e.g., "to initiate a youth employment program in Queenstown").
- Describe activities related to the objectives (e.g., "The Youth Employment Program will increase employment opportunities for youth in Queenstown. . . .").

- Gather information indicating the activities in which partici-pants have actually engaged.
- Gather information that will enable people to judge the extent to which the activities were successful in achieving the purposes of the project or, when purposes have not been achieved or have been poorly achieved, what might account for that poor achievement.
- Engage in processes that enable participants to make judgments about the effectiveness and worth of their activities.

Careful initial planning will facilitate the evaluation process be-cause participants will have clearly defined their activities and the relationship between the activities in which they have engaged and the purposes of the project. Evaluation can sometimes highlight the lack of correspondence between purposes and activities. In the youth employ-ment example given above, for instance, project workers had failed to articulate the relationship between their purposes and the activities in which they had engaged. They rationalized their activities as "provid-ing good role models for unemployed youth," "improving the self-concepts of unemployed youth," and so on. Their activities may or may not have accomplished these objectives, but it is clear that they did little, if anything, to ensure that youth were actually employed. Sometimes, theories—the explanations we give for events and phenomena—are inadequate because they do not fit the reality of people's lives. In this example, the participants may have improved their project by engaging unemployed youth in the process of defining the problem—that is, the reasons they were unemployed—and in finding ways that they could gain employment. Careful processes of evaluation can sometimes re-veal the inadequacies of a research project's initial framing activities.

Celebrating

A good action research project often has no well-defined ending. As people explore their life-worlds together and work toward solutions to their common problems, new realities emerge that extend the processes of inquiry. Problems merge, submerge, or become incorporated into larger projects. Still, there is usually a time when it is possible to stand back, metaphorically speaking, and recognize significant accomplishments. The time for celebrating has arrived.

Celebration is an important part of community-based work. It not only satisfies the human, emotional elements of the experience but also enhances participants' feelings of solidarity, competence, and general well-being. It is a time when the emotional energy expended in particularly difficult activity can be recharged and when any residual antagonisms developed during the project can be defused and relationships among stakeholders enhanced.

Celebrations should reflect the community-based principles of action research as participants get to mingle, talk, and eat and drink together. Music and/or dance will assist the air of celebration, if the context allows it. Formal, sit-down dinners are usually not a good way of celebrating because they anchor people to tables, inhibit interaction, and usually are costly. Buffet lunches or potluck dinners are better, but barbecues, brunches, and other types of parties are equally appropriate ways of celebrating. Any celebration should be held at a time that will maximize the opportunity for all stakeholders, especially those who performed activities, to attend, and in a place where the members of the least powerful groups will feel comfortable.

Speeches should be kept to a minimum, because the purpose of the gathering is to allow participants to celebrate their accomplishments *together*. There should be a time, however, when "significant people" provide a ritualized and formal benediction to the project. Key people from within the process may speak to emphasize the collective accomplishment of all stakeholders and participants.

It may also be appropriate for other significant figures, such as the mayor or other politicians, church leaders, senior managers in government departments and community agencies, local sports heroes, or other important community figures, to contribute. The message from such people should be that the broader community or organization recognizes the participants' accomplishments and contributions.

Speeches that highlight the accomplishments of single individuals and the giving of awards to limited numbers of participants are anathema to community-based processes. When the efforts of a few individu-

als are recognized, those who have made "less significant" contributions may feel their work has been inferior. In some way, all should be
recognized for the contributions they have made to the success of the
project. Celebration is a time when all participants can congregate to
acknowledge their collective achievement and say, in one form or
another, "Look what we have accomplished together."

BOX 7.1
Act: Resolving Complex Problems

Purpose:

To enact procedures for organizing and managing large-scale, complex research processes

Processes:

Manage

> **Plan:** Develop a vision statement, an operational plan, and action plans
>
> **Review:** Examine strengths, weaknesses, opportunities, and threats
>
> **Political processes:** Build cooperative links with interested individuals and groups
>
> **Financial plan:** Construct budgets to account for developmental costs and recurrent costs

Organize

> **Organizational base:** A new or existing organization that provides a base of operations
>
> **Organizational structure:** A structure for coordinating and monitoring people and activities

Guide the research process

> **Leadership:** Provide information and maintain participatory, supportive relationships
>
> **Language:** Use clear language that reflects the values of community-based research
>
> **Decision making:** Engage participatory decision-making processes
>
> **Support:** Act as a resource to monitor and support people's activities

Evaluate

> **Purposes:** Define purposes of the evaluation
>
> **Audience:** Decide which people will be informed of results of the evaluation
>
> **Procedures:** Describe processes for evaluating activities
>
> **Evaluation:** Describe what has been done, what has been achieved, what is still to be done, and issues and/or agendas to be resolved

8

Formal Reports,
Theses,
and Dissertations

Stakeholders who operate from within institutional or organizational contexts often require formally structured reports presenting technical features of the research process and detailed descriptions and analyses of the outcomes of an investigation. Government departments, funding organizations, and universities are examples of institutions likely to require such reports. Because continuing funding of projects, programs, and services often rests on the power of reports, this chapter presents a framework for constructing formal reports that do justice to the rigor and efficacy of community-based action research.

The purpose of formal reports, theses, and dissertations is to communicate the outcomes of inquiry to major institutional stakeholding groups. They speak specifically to an academic or bureaucratic audience and must therefore be presented in forms that are acceptable within these contexts. Because of the status enjoyed by science in the modern world, many organizations, institutions, universities, schools, government departments, and business corporations try to replicate the formats required of experimental scientific research in their reporting procedures. In doing so, however, they often lose significant information or present it in a form that fails to adequately represent the complexity and significance of events or to capture the agonies, achievements, tragedies, and triumphs that constitute the reality of people's lives.

Recent developments in interpretive, action-oriented research differ in significant ways from experimental scientific investigation (see e.g., Denzin, 1989, 1997; Guba, 1990; Lincoln & Guba, 1985) and therefore require somewhat different reporting procedures. This chapter, therefore, suggests a framework for presenting formal reports that not only is true to the principles of community-based action research but also enables individuals, organizations, and community groups to communicate effectively the processes and outcomes of their research and development work to bureaucratic and academic audiences.

I have seen many cases of community groups engaged in effective developmental work that constantly face withdrawal of their funding. They lack the skills or resources to construct reports that enable those who fund their activities to understand what they have achieved or to write proposals that clearly articulate their potentials. I myself have been guilty of failing to provide reports that clearly described my activities in terms meaningful to departmental officers and the guidelines within which they necessarily worked. Although I complained bitterly when funding for my activities was withdrawn, I can see in retrospect that I had failed to keep one of our principal stakeholders clearly informed about my activities.

I have also listened to the agonized accounts of students and colleagues who felt assaulted by comments suggesting "That's not [real] research!" from people who did not understand interpretive or action research processes and the associated procedures and types of outcome. This chapter speaks to people in these situations.

The Research Orientation:
Assumptions of Interpretive Research

The community-based action research presented in this book is derived from interpretive research processes suggested by Denzin (1989, 1997). It is based on the assumption that knowledge inherent in people's everyday, taken-for-granted lives has as much validity and utility as knowledge linked to the concepts and theories of the academic disciplines or bureaucratic policies and procedures. The intent is to concede the limitations of expert knowledge and to acknowledge the competence, experience, understanding, and wisdom of ordinary people. Community-based action research therefore seeks to "give voice" to people who have previously been silent research subjects.

Like other forms of interpretive research, community-based action research seeks to reveal and represent people's experience, providing accounts that enable others to understand how issues and events sit in their daily lives. In the process, researchers provide information that enables those responsible for making policy, managing programs, and delivering services to make more informed judgements about their activities, thus increasing the possibility that their policies, programs, and services might be more appropriate and effective for the people they serve.

Community-based action research differs significantly from the objective, generalizable experimental and survey research that is still the prevailing approach to inquiry in the human and behavioral sciences. The following interpretive assumptions are implicit in community-based approaches to inquiry:

- Studies are usually limited in context, engaging processes of inquiry that focus on a specific issue or problem in a particular context.
- Researchers seek to empower principal stakeholders by engaging them as active participants in all phases of the research project, including planning and implementing processes. It has been described as research *of*, *by*, and *for* the people.
- The principal purpose of the research is to extend people's understanding of an issue by providing detailed, richly described

accounts that reveal the problematic, lived experience of stake-holders and their interpretations of the issue investigated.

- Stakeholder joint accounts, derived from creative processes of negotiation, provide the basis for therapeutic action that works toward resolution of the issue or problem investigated. These processes ensure tangible outcomes of direct benefit to the principal stakeholders.

- Stakeholder perspectives are placed alongside viewpoints found within the academic and bureaucratic literature.

- The ultimate purpose of the research is to make the experience and perspectives of ordinary people directly available to policy-makers, professionals, managers, and administrators, so that more appropriate, effective programs and services can be formulated.

Reports, Theses, and Dissertations

One of the problems that continue to concern me is the extent to which formal reports silence the voices of those of whom they speak. For years now, I have been confounded, especially in my own work, by the inability of official reports to capture the sometimes excruciatingly damaging, damning, or disappointing features of people's lives—or the moments of triumph, small or large, that signal significant, life-changing events. The ponderous language of the reports often obscures the experiences of participants and the significance of events portrayed in the body of the text. As one report notes, "Children playing around raw sewage that flows past their houses is not captured by the words of a government report indicating that 'the sewage system in the community is inadequate.' "

Reports, theses, and dissertations, therefore, have new purposes that differ from those of the traditional objective accounts sanctioned by the scientific community. Recent developments in the research literature suggest new ways of formulating written reports that more effectively represent people's experience. Denzin (1997) points to the need to formulate more evocative accounts that provide empathetic understandings of events and experiences. From this perspective, research reports may look and sound more like fictional works—novels or short stories—than the impersonal, objective accounts common in many official reports.

New ways of writing, however, often are confined by traditional formats that structure reports in ways marginally compatible with the intent of the writer. Although traditional reporting structures associated with experimental science seem incompatible with the narrative forms suggested by experimental ethnographic writing, it is still possible to find ways to fulfill the needs of institutional and bureaucratic audiences while remaining true to the intent of community-based action research.

Box 8.1 compares a framework for organizing experimental and survey research reports with a framework relevant to interpretive, action-oriented inquiry. The intent of the former is to provide concise descriptions of observed relationships between variables, often related to the testing of a null hypothesis. The latter provides the means to present narrative accounts derived from the processes of community-based action research.

The remainder of this chapter presents details of the ways of reporting interpretive, action-oriented research processes. The structure is not prescriptive but suggests one way of organizing outcomes of inquiry that is acceptable to people working in institutional and organizational contexts. Researchers should feel free, therefore, to play creatively with the ideas presented, provided that they remain true to the principles of the interpretive processes presented in this book.

The frameworks that follow were derived from my attempts to assist graduate students in formulating dissertation reports within a large research-oriented university. Because most of the faculty had been trained in experimental and survey research and had little understanding of interpretive or naturalistic inquiry, they were puzzled by the students' apparent inability to formulate research according to the dictums of hypothesis-testing research. The frameworks we designed together enabled university faculty to understand the equivalence of the research reporting procedures and, therefore, to "make sense" of it within their own meaning structures.

I have presented this model in a number of university contexts and received positive feedback from many people, both faculty and students. They have indicated that it provides a simple way of formulating

BOX 8.1
Ways of Organizing Experimental and Interpretive Research Reports

EXPERIMENTAL/SURVEY RESEARCH	INTERPRETIVE/ACTION RESEARCH
Section 1: Introduction The introduction identifies the problem, provides background information, presents the research question(s), and states the hypotheses to be tested.	**Section 1: Focus and Framing** This section identifies the *issue* on which the study is focused and frames it within the social, cultural, and/or physical location of particular groups of people. The *purpose* of the study is defined.
Section 2: Literature Review The literature review presents what is known about the problem and identifies gaps and inconsistencies in the academic literature.	**Section 2: Deconstruction** Existing definitions and interpretations of the problem from within the *academic and institutional literature* are described and critiqued to reveal their underlying assumptions.
Section 3: Methodology The methodology section presents the research design and describes the operationalization of hypotheses, sampling procedures, instrumentation, and procedures for data collection and analysis.	**Section 3: Methodology** This section presents the *philosophical assumptions* of the form of inquiry applied in the study. It also presents details of *research processes,* including procedures for *capturing* multiple personal and self-stories describing participant experiences and *bracketing* procedures that identify key elements, features, structures, and themes.
Section 4: Results The results section presents the outcomes of the study, revealing and interpreting the results of data analysis.	**Section 4: Construction** The bracketed elements are classified, ordered, and reassembled into coherent, detailed accounts that present participants' experience and interpretations of events. Accounts provide an empathetic *understanding* of participants' lived experience of the issue investigated.
Section 5: Conclusion The conclusion discusses the theoretical and practical implications of the study, sometimes also presenting recommendations for applying the results of the study.	**Section 5: Contextualization** Participant perspectives are *relocated in the broader social context* by comparing and contrasting their accounts with existing academic and institutional interpretations of the issue. The section also explores the *implications* of the study for policies, programs, and practices related to the issue.

Action research incorporates another phase of research activity, wherein accounts lead to actions that become incorporated into the content of Section 4 of the report.

a research report that is acceptable to the evaluative requirements of university life.

Section 1: Focus and Framing

Section 1 presents an overview that enables readers to understand why the study was instituted and the issue on which it is focused. It frames the study by locating it within the boundaries of a particular social context and prepares readers for the rest of the report. It describes the following:

- The issue or problem on which the investigation focuses
- The specific physical location(s) of the investigation and the principal stakeholding groups
- Organizations, policies, programs, and services affecting the issue in the local context
- The purposes of the research
- The significance of the study
- The content of each section and/or chapter of the report

Section 2: Deconstructing the Literature

The purpose of the second section is to help readers understand the ways in which writers of official documents and academic literature have interpreted the issue investigated. These perspectives are deconstructed, or taken apart, to reveal the concepts, theories, and underlying assumptions on which their various claims and viewpoints are based. This process digs below the surface of the reports to reveal the implicit systems of knowledge (discourses) and cultural practices embedded in the theoretical literature and in social programs and services.

The process of deconstruction requires a review of viewpoints presented in the literature of

- *The academic disciplines:* Academic texts, research reports, and academic journals
- *The professions:* Publications and journals of professional bodies, such as teachers' unions, social worker associations, public service journals, and so on
- *Government agency policies and programs:* Parliamentary records, legislation, departmental documents, policy papers, annual reports, research reports, sectional reports, client service literature, reviews, evaluations, procedural manuals, and so on
- *Organizations and institutions:* Organizational literature from schools, hospitals, clinics, centers, churches, businesses, and so on, including policies, plans, strategies, evaluations, reports, procedural manuals, curricula, public relations literature, informational literature, and so forth
- *Media:* News articles, feature reports, and documentaries in newspapers, journals, magazines, films, and television

The review and deconstruction of this literature set the stage for a later process (see Section 5) in which official and academic viewpoints are compared and contrasted with research participant perspectives.

Section 3: Methodology

Section 3 presents a rationale for the approach to research used in the study (philosophical assumptions) and describes in detail the way it was conducted (research processes). It is designed to inform readers why this approach to research was chosen as appropriate to the issue investigated and to indicate that it was a rigorous process of investigation.

Methodological Assumptions: A Philosophical Rationale

Because interpretive, action-oriented approaches to inquiry have been accepted only recently as legitimate in academic and official settings, the first subsection may require a more extended treatment than is expected of experimental or survey research reports. It provides information that identifies the research paradigm and provides readers with details of the purposes, processes, and outcomes of naturalistic or interpretive research. In doing so, it is useful to cite sources that enable readers to extend their understanding of the paradigm (e.g., Denzin & Lincoln, 1994; Guba, 1990; Guba & Lincoln, 1989).

This subsection should implicitly answer these questions: "Why have we used this approach to research?" and "Is it a valid and rigorous research process?" It may be helpful to clarify the nature of the research process by comparing and contrasting naturalistic or interpretive inquiry with the experimental and survey research that is often presented in academic and bureaucratic reports. It is useful to know the extent to which intended readers value and have experience with interpretive, action research.

Some years ago, I presented a report to a government department that evaluated one of its programs. When I formally presented the report, the head of the department informed me rather frostily that "this is not an evaluation!" Although I thought I had negotiated details of the evaluation prior to accepting the contract, the departmental officers responsible had moved on to other positions. Their replacements did not understand the nature of the report I had written, in part because of my own failure to describe the nature of my approach to inquiry in my report. I now know that I should have clearly articulated what readers could expect as outcomes of the research process. More specifically, however, I should have communicated that to the new people who had assumed responsibility for the evaluation.

Research Processes

The second subsection provides readers with details of the way the study was carried out. It enables them to clearly understand how researchers went about the work of investigating the issue, including who was involved, what information was collected, and how the information was analyzed. This section would be called "the research design" in experimental and survey research.

Position of the Researcher

It is especially important to describe and explain the role of the research facilitator. Readers should understand how the relationship between the research facilitator and other participants helped shape the processes and outcomes of the investigation. The researcher may be described as a consultant, resource person, scribe, or coparticipant whose role is to assist people, rather than control them. The research is done *with* the people, not *on* or *about* them. This section is relevant to the general interpretive purpose of representing the experience and perspective of participants and to the values inherent in community-based action research.

Participants

Readers should be informed of the number and type of people who participate in the investigation. The term *participant* is a departure from the term *subject* normally used in experimental and survey research and reflects a change in the status and role of people involved. Participants in community-based action research actively engage in monitoring and directing the processes of inquiry.

The type and number of people who participate in the research should be explicitly identified so that readers will clearly understand the sources of information. Researchers particularly need to identify the principal stakeholders—those who have most at stake in the issue—and other important groups who have contributed to the study.

In a school-related project, students and parents were identified as the principal stakeholders. Other significant stakeholders included the principal of the school and other principals in the district, teachers, and the district superintendent. Information from these sources enabled research facilitators to build an understanding of how the issue affected the lives of the students and their parents and how the issue fit into the local school context.

Capture: Information
(Data) Collection Techniques

As discussed in Chapter 4, this subsection describes the type of information acquired and how it was recorded. It is sometimes useful to cite authors who have suggested those procedures, for example, "This study used interviewing/data collection/data analysis procedures suggested by Spradley (1979). Initial open-ended questions that enabled participants to describe and interpret experiences in their own terms were complemented by . . ." The following types of detail may be included:

- *Interviews:* The type of interviewing procedures used, with whom, number and duration of interviews, during what period, and where and when interviews occurred
- *Observations:* Activities, events, or locations observed, related to which people, how, at what time, for how long (or actors, acts, activities, events, objects, places, and times)
- *Documents, media, and artifacts:* Documents, official reports, minutes, procedures, materials, policies, letters, records, and so on, that were scrutinized; films, videos, and media reports reviewed; artwork, working papers, and other objects produced by participants; samples; and so on
- *Recording information:* How information was recorded—field notes, audio- and videotapes, photographs, photocopies, and so on

Bracketing: Interpretive Procedures
for Analyzing Data

This subsection provides readers with an understanding of the ways that research participants analyzed or interpreted information. *Bracketing* is a term used in interpretive research to refer to the process of analyzing information to reduce it to its most significant, or key, elements.

Interpretive inquiry typically produces large masses of information that has limited use in its raw form. Established procedures enable researchers to reduce, condense, or distill this mass of information so that significant features of people's experience become available in a readily accessible form. This subsection describes details of procedures used for this reduction process—for selecting, categorizing, and labeling information. In general, these forms of analysis establish categories and key elements of experience that provide the framework and content of accounts that emerge in the body of the report (see Section 4 below). A wide range of analytic procedures now have currency within the academic world (e.g., Denzin, 1989; Lincoln & Guba, 1985), so that readers need to clearly understand how interpretive procedures (data analysis) relate to the processes and products of investigation.

▦ Rigor

This section provides readers with evidence that the research has been carried out rigorously, that the procedures and processes of inquiry have minimized the possibility that the investigation was superficial, biased, or insubstantial. Traditional criteria for evaluating the rigor of experimental and survey research—objectivity, reliability, validity, and generalizability—are inappropriate in naturalistic inquiry. Lincoln and Guba (1985) suggest a different set of criteria for establishing rigor in interpretive inquiry.

Researchers may therefore establish the trustworthiness of their study by reporting on the following:

- *Credibility* is established by *prolonged engagement* with participants; *triangulation* of information from multiple data sources; *member checking* procedures that allow participants to check and verify the accuracy of the information recorded; and *peer debriefing* processes that enable research facilitators to articulate and reflect on research procedures with a colleague or informed associate.

- *Transferability* is established by describing the means for applying the research findings to other contexts. Fundamentally, the possibility of applying findings across settings is established through thickly detailed descriptions that enable audiences to identify similarities of the research setting with other contexts.

Put another way, it enables other audiences to see themselves and/or their situations in the accounts presented.

- *Dependability and confirmability* are provided through an audit trail that clearly describes the processes of collecting and analyzing data and provides the means by which readers may refer to the raw data.

Limitations

Researchers should indicate any limitations that arose from the pragmatic realities of investigation. It is not usually possible to include all the people who should be included, to interview them for the extended periods warranted by interpretive inquiry, to follow up on all relevant issues, and to deal with all the contingencies that arise. Human inquiry, like any other human activity, is both complex and always incomplete. We need to acknowledge the extent of that incompleteness in accounts we write of our work.

This section is not an apology for failing to live up to the criteria of experimental investigation. Why these criteria for rigor (objectivity, reliability, and so on) are not appropriate should have been covered in the methodology section of the report.

Ethical Issues

In the past, researchers have taken for granted the right to acquire information from people and to use it for their own purposes. Many groups who have been subjects of research now refuse to allow access to outside researchers. As a participatory approach to investigation, community-based action research therefore confronts ethical issues rarely acknowledged in other types of study. This section of the report describes steps taken by research facilitators to maintain the rights and privacy of research participants, including procedures that guard against unwarranted intrusion into their lives, maintain their privacy, and establish appropriate ownership and uses of the products of investigation. It may also describe how research processes were enacted in ways sensitive to the cultural values and protocols of research participants.

Section 4: Constructing Accounts:
Research Outcomes or Results

Section 4 is often described as the "results" section of the report, enabling researchers to present what they have discovered in their investigation. Unlike experimental research that usually reports on observed relationships between variables, interpretive research presents narrative accounts that reveal the ways people experience the issue investigated and the context within which it is held. It presents richly detailed, thickly described accounts that enable readers to empathetically understand the lived reality of research participants. These accounts are constructed from information collected and analyzed during the study (cf. Section 3). They should include the perspectives of people from all major stakeholding groups.

Interpretive procedures described in the previous section provide bracketed elements (significant features of experience) that are classified, ordered, and reassembled into detailed, coherent accounts. These accounts

- *Describe* events, activities, and contexts from the perspective of the participants. This may include sequential accounts of events and acts, activities, objects, times, places, purposes, and emotions relevant to the issue investigated.
- Present the way participants *interpret* events, activities, and so on, including how things occur and explanations for those occurrences (why they occurred as they did).

Setting the Scene

As with any story, readers need to understand where the story is set, the people involved, and other relevant background information. One way of organizing this section of the account is to first set the scene and then move on to tell the stories that have emerged. Another method is to begin with individual stories, weaving in descriptions of the setting as the person's story emerges. The purpose, at this stage, is to present a more detailed account extending the general information provided in Section 1. Descriptions should reflect participant views of the setting, rather than the "objective" voice of the researcher, so that accounts ring with participant voices, using their concepts and their language to describe the people and the setting. Any of the following *descriptive features* might be included:

- *Actors:* People who are significant or relevant to the story
- *Acts and activities:* The things people do; activities in which they engage
- *Events:* Significant events or incidents that take place
- *Place:* Where those activities or events take place
- *Time:* When they occur and for how long
- *Purpose:* What people are trying to accomplish; why they do what they do
- *Emotion:* How they feel about what happens, what they do
- *Objects:* Buildings, goods, materials, clothes, cars, books, reports, and so on

In "setting the scene," writers should focus on those features of the situation that appear important from the participants' perspectives. They enable readers to see the context through the eyes of the participants and to understand their perspective. In some instances, large chunks of data may be included in the text to strengthen this process.

Constructing Accounts: Telling People's Stories

It is common reporting practice to formulate generalized accounts by combining information acquired from a number of individuals or groups. The problem with generalized accounts is that they fail to capture the lived reality, the actual on-the-ground experience of the people whose lives they are reporting. By aggregating the data, report writers risk losing those significant events or features of experience that really make a difference in their lives. A method more appropriate to an action-oriented, interpretive approach to research commences with stories of individuals. This case study approach endeavors to capture and represent individual experience more directly by focusing on events that have a significant impact on their lives—*epiphanic* events that reveal the significance of events related in reports.

Bill Genat (1998) provides an example of this process in the way he frames the story of Aboriginal health workers. He presents stories on a number of workers, each account illuminating different features of health workers' experiences. One story is titled "Powerlessness: An Account of Ruby's Experience" (fictitious name). He commences with a quote that powerfully captures a moment of crisis:

> They wanted all us healthworkers, 'cause we were going to change everything, but we're so strictly dictated to, it's changed nothing—some of us have great ideas, and we could do it all, but we just can't do it—instead of like, handing things to us—we're always dictated to. . . . We don't get enough say in the programme. . . . I thought, yes, we've got a power, we're united, but then last week it just killed it. . . . We say we want to have our own voice!—you should'a been there—there was all these powerful health-workers that just agreed to everything [the nurse] said. . . . People are still dying—Teddy's going to get his toes cut off—Daisy died. . . . People are just dying of things that could have been changed. . . .

Genat then provides an account of events that surround that crisis, focusing on those features of the situation that enable readers to understand how a particular set of events sits in the experience of that health worker.

Epiphanies:
Moments of Crisis or Triumph

Epiphanic events are moments of crisis or triumph—turning-point moments that have the potential to be transformational. Reports that focus on epiphanies illuminate important features of people's experience and provide readers with a much more substantial understanding of their lives. They may reveal significant problematic events and behaviors that shatter people's lives or continuing, underlying tensions and problems that cumulatively erode their well-being. Conversely, they may provide uplifting accounts that reveal how people's lives have been enhanced by gratifying events or visionary experiences.

The following elements provide the basis for constructing an account focusing on epiphanic experiences:

- *Key people:* Select individuals who represent in significant ways those who constitute the various stakeholding groups. Commence with people from the primary stakeholding group.

- *Epiphany:* For each individual, review all relevant information (data) and select an event or events that the person has indicated to be significant—moments of crisis or triumph.

- *Moment of crisis:* For each event, identify a few paragraphs of talk in which the person describes the "crisis point," the defining moment of the crisis event, in his or her own words. Commence by quoting that piece of data.

- *Defining features:* From the data, identify additional features of the situation that seem important, from the perspective of the person. Code and categorize those features if necessary.

- *Headings:* Use the resulting categories as a framework of headings to extend the person's story, so that the reader can understand (a) the nature of the crisis and (b) the way that crisis sits in the person's everyday life.

As the story emerges, use *descriptive features* (e.g., actors, acts, and activities; see above) that seem most suited to illuminating the person's experience. Focus on those aspects of the context that are significant from the person's perspective, rather than on commentary derived from others. Accomplish a story that the person would recognize as his or her experience and perspective.

Accounts should provide sufficient material to enable intended audiences to understand the experience and perspectives primarily of key people in the primary stakeholding group. The stories that emerge in the report also provide understandings of the ways that other significant stakeholders experience the issue investigated. A report of an investigation of school dropouts not only would focus on the perspectives and experiences of students who left school early but also should provide an understanding of the perspectives of peers, teachers, parents, school administrators, and others having a stake in the issue.

Constructing a General Account

Most reports contain a general account that summarizes what has been discovered from the processes of investigation. It provides an opportunity to understand the issue in ways that enable participants to work toward a resolution of the problem(s) on which the research has focused. The next phase of the reporting process provides this type of account.

Once individual accounts have been formulated, list the key features that formed the basis for each account and review them. Categorize the features according to previously described procedures. That is, identify features or themes that are common to all or a number of the stories. Names or headings may differ, but they may refer to similar features; for example, "arguing," "fighting," and "criticizing" might be parts of the category "conflict." More extended descriptions of this process are provided in Chapters 4 and 5.

After those features or themes are identified, organize them into headings and subheadings that provide the framework for a narrative that tells how groups of people experience the issue being investigated. Accounts will focus on experiences and perspectives that people have in common but may also refer to the different perspectives people have of events. At this time, do not explore, analyze, critique, or otherwise comment on their experience. The intent at this stage is to reveal and accept nonjudgmentally and uncritically the ways people describe and interpret their experience.

Section 5: Contextualizing: Concluding Comments

Whereas the previous section presented accounts of participants' experiences and perspectives, this final section places those experiences and perspectives in a broader context. This is the "so what" section of a formal report or dissertation that enables writers to articulate newly emerging understandings of the issue and to compare and contrast them with perspectives that exist in the academic literature or bureaucratic documentation. In effect, it presents succinctly what has been discovered and explores the implications of those findings. This section does the following:

- Summarizes the outcomes of the study
- Places stakeholder viewpoints in the broader social context of the issue by comparing and contrasting their perspectives with those presented within the literature
- Explores the implications of the study for policies, programs, services, and practices related to the people and the issue investigated
- Suggests actions that may be initiated or extended, or modifications of activities and/or procedures that will improve existing programs or services

Its purpose is to show clearly how stakeholder perspectives illuminate the issue investigated and to suggest changes in organizational or programmatic practices implied by the outcomes of the research. In the academic world, it may also propose ways that existing theoretical perspectives are enhanced or challenged by the new understandings emerging from the research process.

I was involved in a project that investigated the training needs of workers in a human services agency. The research clearly revealed the type of skills and knowledge required and suggested ways that skills development training could be organized. A review of existing literature on adult education and the human resources procedures of the agency augmented this information. It was creative work, requiring careful planning that encompassed the training needs revealed in the research process within the human resource development procedures of the agency. This resulted in a powerful training program that in the long term significantly enhanced the capabilities of the agency.

Giving Voice: Alternative Report Structures

I have previously alluded to the need to develop more effective means for communicating the outcomes of research and development work. I have suggested a variety of ways in which the knowledge, understanding, and the more pragmatic outcomes of our research efforts might be represented, including poems, dramas, narratives, fiction, memoirs, autobiographies, autoethnographies, film, and so on. This requires us to draw on and develop literary devices that are able to evoke more clearly the deeply felt and experienced realities of people's day-to-day lives.

Apart from the style and nature of the language used in reports, however, their very structure often inhibits the clear and adequate representation of people's experiences and perspectives. This has recently become clear to me as I have helped people write formal dissertations. The report structure presented above engages both author and reader in an extensive discussion, first of the study itself, then the literature related to the issue, and finally the methodology and research processes. By the time readers arrive at the heart of the report, they have waded through many pages of writing that provide essentially background information. The voices of the principal stakeholders have become muted and sometimes lost in the academic or bureaucratic issues that tend to predominate in reports of this variety.

With my colleagues, I have recently commenced to work creatively to modify the structure of formal reports so that the experience and the voice of the research participants remains clearly in the forefront of the document. The frameworks in Box 8.2 are adapted from those presented in the first sections of this chapter. Although they require some modifications and adaptations to the content of some sections, the rearrangement seems more clearly suited to an approach to research seeking to give voice to the people.

The objective of these report structures is to provide ways of reporting that focus on the central objective of a report—the perspective of the principal stakeholders. The intent is to ensure that the most important information derived from the processes of inquiry—the perspectives, agendas, experiences, interests, and ideas of research participants—are given greatest prominence.

<table>
<tr><td colspan="2" align="center">**Box 8.2**
Alternative Research Report Structures</td></tr>
<tr><td>**REPORT STRUCTURE 1**</td><td>**REPORT STRUCTURE 2**</td></tr>
<tr><td>**Section 1: Introduction**

Research purpose, focus, context, and participants
Brief synopsis of the methodology
The nature and structure of the report, including a brief synopsis of each chapter</td><td>**Section 1: Introduction**

Same as Structure 1</td></tr>
<tr><td>**Section 2: Deconstruction/ Literature Review**

Description and critique of existing perspectives from academic and bureaucratic literature</td><td>**Section 2: Results/Accounts**

Accounts reveal the ways participants describe and interpret their experience of the issue studied</td></tr>
<tr><td>**Section 3: Results/Accounts**

Accounts reveal the ways in which participants describe and interpret their experience of the issue studied</td><td>**Section 3: Deconstruction/ Literature Review**

Description and critique of existing perspectives from academic and bureaucratic literature</td></tr>
<tr><td>**Section 4: Contextualization**

Contrasts and comments on the differing perspectives presented in the results section and the literature review; suggests implications for policies, programs, and professional practices</td><td>**Section 4: Contextualization**

Contrasts and comments on the differing perspectives presented in the results section and the literature review; suggests implications for policies, programs, and professional practices</td></tr>
<tr><td>**Appendix: Methodology and Research Process**

Describes the research paradigm and gives details of research processes</td><td>**Appendix: Methodology and Research Process**

Describes the research paradigm and gives details of research processes</td></tr>
</table>

Structure 1, therefore, removes the methodological section from its prominent place in the report and places it as an appendix in the rear of the report. This change removes a potentially lengthy technical discussion from the body of the report, placing it in a less intrusive position in the text, while still providing that information for audiences who may be concerned about the technical features of the research process.

When Structure 1 is used, the report needs to expand the first section a little to include basic information about the nature of the report. This will inform readers of the nature of research that has been carried out and the type of results they might expect in the report. If people read a report expecting to see results in the form of causes and effects depicted as variables accompanied by tables of frequencies, they may not orient their reading to the type of text presented or realize the consequence of the report.

Structure 2 takes this process a step further, removing the sometimes intrusive voices of bureaucratic and academic research reports as the frame for research participant perspectives. Thus the outcomes of the research process are reported in Section 2, leaving discussion of the literature for the following section. This enables the literature to be reviewed in light of the perspectives emerging from the research process, thus conceding the limitations of expert knowledge and emphasizing the primary relevance of the experience and know-how of people in their everyday lives.

The commonalities and differences between participant perspectives emerging in the study and the perspectives on the issue reported in the literature become one of the focal points of Section 4. We are, in effect, exploring the implications of the outcomes of the study. Where the outcomes concur with perspectives in the literature, we are able to validate, to some degree, our findings; where research outcomes are at odds with perspectives within the literature, we can explore the implications of the situation. Some people suggest that the literature review section of the report be deleted altogether, perspectives from the research literature being introduced only in the final section in counterpoint to the major findings of the research and as a point of discussion for its implications.

Understanding Action Research

THE THEORY BEHIND THE PRACTICE

Previous chapters in this book have presented one cycle of an action research process in a linear fashion. In practice, the look, think, and act phases not only are reiterative but tend to fold into each other as people review and reflect on the events and activities in which they are involved. An important feature of an action research process, however, is that participants not remain doggedly true to a stipulated recipe but keep track of the different activities in which they engage, working systematically through the information and ideas that emerge.

In this final chapter, I will review and reflect on the processes described in the preceding chapters. This is an opportunity for us—author and reader—to think about the nature and purposes of the work in which we have been engaged—to practice the reflective processes embedded in the "look, think, act" routine. In so doing, we can inspect those processes in light of the understandings that emerged as we integrated new ways of thinking and doing into our worldview and cross-pollinate that new knowledge with the realities of our current situation. By reflecting on our new knowledge, we can probe or analyze its strength and utility by testing it, in our minds, against the reality of our everyday experience.

As I reflect on community-based action research, I find that I tend to compare and contrast this new method of investigation with older, more traditional paradigms of scientific research; with postmodern social theory; and with my own experience in teaching and working in universities, schools, government agencies, and community settings in Australia, the United States, and Great Britain. Readers—because of the differing ways in which we all approach the reading of any type of text—will interpret and explore the processes of community-based action research according to the paradigms and contexts that are part of your own experiences. This process, if it is successful, will generate in you, the reader, new ways of thinking about research and stimulate you to explore further ways to extend your understanding of your professional and community life.

Community-Based Research Revisited

Community-based research starts, as does all research, with a problem to be solved. Unlike positivistic science, however, its goal is not the production of an objective body of knowledge that can be generalized to large populations. Instead, its purpose is to build collaboratively constructed descriptions and interpretations of events that enable groups of people to formulate mutually acceptable solutions to their problems. Community-based research, however, recognizes that any research process has multiple outcomes and takes into account the need to enact ways of working that protect or enhance the dignity and identities of all people involved. It is oriented toward ways of organizing and enacting professional and community life that are democratic, equitable, liberating, and life enhancing.

The approach to inquiry that I have presented may appear somewhat idealistic. Competitive social values, impersonal work practices, and authoritarian modes of control impose themselves as constant conditions of our work. Institutionalized practices—those commonly accepted as "the way things are done"—seem so pervasive and normal that we often cannot envisage other ways of working, even when those practices are ineffective or, in some cases, detrimental to our purposes.

I once engaged in a study of classrooms by observing three primary school classes for a year. Although at that time, I had been a classroom teacher for almost 10 years, the study dramatically changed my vision of schools. My discovery that children spent extended periods passively watching or listening resulted in a significant change in my perspective. As a classroom teacher, my vision of classrooms was one in which there was a constant and sometimes almost overwhelming flow of activity. I was astounded that young children were forced to cope with long periods of inactivity during which they were permitted only to watch and listen as the teacher interacted with other individuals. That experience changed my perception of classroom life quite fundamentally, so that I am now much more sensitive to the passivity that is a pervasive feature of school life and to the need to engage students constantly in active learning processes.

The pressures of bureaucratic life, the limitations of resources, and the competitive push for career advancement consistently work against attempts to humanize and democratize research processes. Community-based procedures that highlight the active participation of people in formulating and controlling research activities and events are hard to attain and difficult to maintain. When they can be achieved, however, they provide a powerful means of accomplishing any set of social or professional goals. The act of observing and reflecting on our own practices can be an enlightening experience, enabling us to see ourselves more clearly and to formulate ways of working that are more effective and that enhance the lives of the people with whom we work. Collaborative processes not only generate a sense of purpose and energy but also provide the means for the accomplishment of goals and the solution of problems and produce conditions that enhance participants' personal, social, and professional lives.

"But It's Not Scientific":
The Question of Legitimacy

Although action research is gaining increased support in the professional community, it has yet to be accepted by many academic researchers as a legitimate form of inquiry. From time to time, practitioners who engage in action research will find themselves subject to the negative comments, sometimes quite vitriolic, of people who do not regard such work as genuine research because "it's not scientific." A recent proposal for a paper on action research that I submitted for presentation at a national educational research conference, for instance, was rejected after one reviewer commented, "There may be a place for this nonsense in AERA, but not, hopefully, in this [the research] division."

It may be worthwhile, therefore, to spend a little time here exploring issues related to action research, so that those who enact it may rest easy in the knowledge that despite such comments and questions, action research is a legitimate, authentic, and rigorous approach to inquiry. Fuller treatments of this debate are provided in a number of other books (e.g., Lincoln & Guba's *Naturalistic Inquiry*, 1985), but an overview will at least provide a basic understanding of the nature of the issues to be addressed.

I have personally studied the issues related to the different forms of social research for more than 20 years. In that time, I have become aware that the field is sufficiently contentious to engage the attention of some of the world's leading scholars. The debate is far from concluded, although the weight of argument seems to suggest that what has traditionally been accepted as scientific research is but one of a number of legitimate approaches to academic and professional inquiry.

Whether action research is accepted as scientific depends on the way in which *science* is defined. Certainly it is, in one sense, rigorously empirical, insofar as it requires people to define clearly and observe the phenomena under investigation. Evident also, however, is that action research does not follow the carefully prescribed procedures that have become inscribed as *scientific method.*

Scientific method seeks to test theories that purport to explain why or how the world is as it is. The ultimate aim is to derive lawlike statements that explain the nature of the world or the nature of reality. Scientific method seeks to generate knowledge that is *objective* (not amenable to the subjective or authoritative judgments of individuals, organizations, or institutions) and *generalizable* (applicable to a wide variety of contexts). It must also be *reliable* (the results should be replicable by any person similarly placed) and *valid* (it should describe a "true" state of affairs). The laws of science seek to provide invariant forms of knowledge that enable us to predict future events on the basis of a preexisting set of conditions. In recent history, this ability to predict and therefore control many facets of the physical world has provided humanity with the ability to manipulate the environment to an unprecedented degree. The technological miracles of the modern world are a testament to the power of knowledge derived from the application of the scientific method.

The success of scientific forms of inquiry in the physical world, however, has not been mirrored in investigations of human behavior and the social world. Except to the extent that humans are physical beings, scientific investigation has largely failed to provide a social equivalent of the comparatively stable body of knowledge about the physical universe. A science of humanity, social life, or individual behavior has failed to emerge within anthropology, sociology, or psychology, despite the huge resources poured into research in these disciplines in the past few decades. Human beings, it seems, are hard to predict and difficult to control.

Two major factors account for the failure of the scientific method to provide a set of laws for human behavior and social life. First, scientific knowledge is now recognized to be much less stable, objective, and generalizable than previously assumed and, therefore, is less secure as a basis for formulating human action. Second, there is increasing acceptance of the fundamental difference between the nature of the social world and that of the physical world. Although it has been relatively easy to accept the notion of a fixed reality that could be "discovered" in the physical universe, the social universe is now recognized as a continually changing cultural creation. Social reality exists as an unstable and dynamic construction that is fabricated, maintained, and modified by people during their interaction with each other and their environment. It operates according to systems of meaning embedded in each cultural context and can be understood only superficially without reference to those meanings.

Investigation of the social and behavioral worlds cannot be operationalized in scientific terms because the phenomena to be tested lack the stability required by traditional scientific method. Humans are, to a large extent, what they define themselves to be in any given situation.

So where does this leave those people who wish to investigate human affairs with the intent that they should provide knowledge that will "make a difference" to people's lives? In the past, it has been accepted that "experts," or those who are authorized by credentials that signal their access to scientific knowledge, should provide answers to social problems. Researchers are becoming increasingly aware of the limitations of this perspective, however. Scientific knowledge is partial, incomplete, and reductionist (i.e., it reduces phenomena to minute components) and is often of limited practical use.

Professionals armed with limited scientific formulations and theories about human behavior tend to prescribe behavior or action according to routines, recipes, values, and perceptions derived from their own histories and cultural experiences or according to the institutional imperatives of the organizational contexts within which they work. As a result, programs and services often fail to do the jobs intended; in some cases, they merely aggravate the problems they are meant to remediate. Programs and services, especially those for marginalized groups, frequently fail to recognize the reality of people's lives and implicitly deny the strengths that are an inherent part of their community and family lives. From the perspective of recipients, "helping" services and programs are often accompanied by degrees of implicit criticism and control that attack their very humanity.

I have had the good fortune to work with Aboriginal people in Western Australia for many years. The strength and vitality of their family and community lives, which I experience in a continuing way as I work with various groups in organizational and community contexts, is belied by the perspectives presented to me when I teach classes of teachers, social workers, and health professionals. There is a tendency for people in these contexts to focus on that minority of Aboriginal people who capture the sensationalizing gaze of the media, to generalize from that group to all Aboriginal people, and to fail to recognize and value the contributions of the many solid and hardworking persons who make up the majority of the Aboriginal community. Professionals tend to approach Aboriginal people with the intent of "helping" them, or as people in need of "training." They talk of the "cultural deficits" of Aboriginal children and the need for Aboriginal people to learn "social skills." Their ethnocentrism would be merely annoying if it were not that many of them are in positions of professional power that permit them to have significant impacts on the lives of people for whom they have so little regard. Aboriginal people often find their lives controlled by experts and public servants who have little understanding of their social and cultural realities and are apt to act in ways that are inappropriate or demeaning from an Aboriginal perspective.

I am once again reminded of the words of the Aboriginal social worker Lilla Watson: "If you've come to help me, you're wasting your time. But if you've come because your liberation is bound up with mine, then let us work together."

Power, Control, and Subordination

A significant feature of modern societies is the increased access to goods and services available to people through centralized processes of mass production and bureaucratic organization. The increased efficiencies gained through the large-scale organization of activity are accompanied by demands for more effective control to ensure the most effective possible use of resources. One of the fictions of modern management is that scientific planning procedures may be used to describe objectives, activities, and outcomes in precise detail, a continuing source of frustration for those who work in large organizations—government departments and agencies, educational institutions, health services, community organizations, and so on.

One result of this dynamic is that teachers, social workers, clerical staff, and other professional workers are subject to increasing levels of stress as restrictive legislative mandates and administrative controls attempt to dictate precisely the ways they enact their professional duties. Managers and administrators of programs and services are often subject to even greater stress, caught in the nexus of organizational imperatives, recalcitrant subordinates and clients, the complex reality of the social contexts they engage, and their personal needs for ego satisfaction and career advancement. Highly prescriptive plans provide little opportunity for managers and practitioners to adapt and adjust their work to the realities of the particular environments in which they operate and act to increase the levels of anxiety associated with their work.

The problem is, of course, that it is impossible to control human behavior with the rigor and precision demanded by the procedures of the physical sciences. The dynamism of social life and the creative and willful facets of human behavior prevent the high degrees of control that are embedded in scientific method and technological production. Attempts to impose the same type and extent of control in the delivery of human services have led to increasing levels of stress and alienation as practitioners struggle to provide necessary services within the boundaries of increasingly restrictive policies and procedural rules.

I rarely meet a friend or colleague who is "happy in the service" these days. Those who work in human service agencies or organizations as practitioners or managers frequently complain about the unrealistic demands and excessive numbers of directives that inhibit the effective accomplishment of their work. The complaints cover all fields, from social work through education and health to community and youth work. The quality of professional life appears to be diminishing as demands for greater control and accountability increase.

How, then, are we to understand the events that make up our lives? Behavioral theorists focus on the capabilities and characteristics of individuals and point to factors such as motivation, achievement need, intelligence, and cognition to explain people's behavior. Social theorists, on the other hand, tend to stress the large-scale forces—class, gender, race, and ethnicity—that determine social events. Marxist-oriented theorists, for instance, explain social events by the controlling and competitive relationships inherent in modern capitalist economic systems. The people who control the means of production, this genre of theory suggests, maintain systems of domination that reinforce the power and authority of those in positions of power at the expense of subordinate groups.

Although these theories are interesting and useful for some purposes, they are limited in their applicability to the problems experienced by individuals and social groups in their day-to-day lives. If we accept the economic determinism inherent in Marxist theory, for example, we are but puppets on the world stage, our lives ordered by the workings of the international economic order, our efforts to improve our lives essentially fruitless.

A recent genre of theory, known collectively as *postmodern*, provides a distinctive way of envisioning the social world that enables us to understand human experience in different ways. Although modern perspectives of the world are bound to scientific visions of a fixed and knowable world, postmodernism questions the nature of social reality and the very processes by which we can come to know about it. Elements of postmodernism suggest that knowledge can no longer be accepted as an objective set of testable truths because it is produced by processes that are inherently "captured" by features of the social world it seeks to explain. Scientists, as products of particular historical and cultural experiences, will formulate explanations of the social world that derive from their own experiences and hence tend to validate their own perceptual universes.

From a postmodern perspective, attempts to order people's lives on the basis of scientific knowledge largely constitute an exercise in power. Knowledge, and the research that produces that knowledge, is as much about politics as it is about understanding. An understanding of what research is about is not just an exploration of method but an inquiry into the ways in which knowledge is produced and the benefits that accrue to people who control the processes of knowledge production.

The theoretical discourse that follows is not presented as a description of "the" social world. It is articulated as one way of interpreting social experience and presents perspectives that seem to make sense from my viewpoint. In essence, I, as author, provide a framework of ideas that is a rationale for community-based action research. Those readers who find it unhelpful may choose to skip the next passage and formulate their own rationale for accepting or rejecting the approach to research that I advocate.

Understanding Power and Control: Postmodern Perspectives

Postmodern theory derives much of its power from the way it deconstructs—that is, pulls apart for examination—mechanisms of knowledge production. Scientific rationality, a key feature of modern organizational life, has itself become subject to forms of philosophical investigation that raise doubts about many of the taken-for-granted assumptions on which our understandings of the social and physical universe rest. An exploration of postmodern perspectives, therefore, assists us to extend our understanding of the frustrations experienced by practitioners as they work in social, community, and organizational contexts.

Michel Foucault's (1972) exploration of social life, for instance, reinforces the notion that there can be no objective truth because there is an essential relationship between the ways in which knowledge is produced and the way power is exercised. Foucault's study of the development of modern institutional life led him to conclude that there is an intimate relation between the systems of knowledge ("discourses") by which people arrange their lives and the techniques and practices through which social control and domination are exercised in local contexts. Humans are subject to oppression, Foucault suggests, not only because of the operation of large-scale systems of control and authority but also because of the normally accepted procedures, routines, and practices through which we enact our daily public and personal lives.

From a Foucauldian perspective, such institutional sites as schools, agency offices, hospitals, clinics, and youth centers might be viewed as examples of places where a dispersed and piecemeal organization of power is built up independent of any systematic strategy of domination. What happens in these contexts cannot be understood by focusing only on systemwide strategies of control. At each site, a professional elite, which includes administrators, researchers and teachers, social workers, nurses, doctors, and youth workers, defines the language and the discourse and, in doing so, builds a framework of meaning into the organization and operation of the system. Individual members of this elite exert control by contributing to the framing and maintenance of ordinary, commonly accepted practices, which are often enshrined in bureaucratic fiat, administrative procedure, or government regulation. The end point of this process is the accrual of "profit" to people in a position to define the "codes of knowledge" that form the basis for organizational life. Professional acceptance, employment, promotion, funding, and other forms of recognition provide a system of rewards for people able to influence or reinforce definitions inscribed in reports, regulations, rules, policies, procedures, curricula, texts, and professional literature.

Foucault (1972) contends that any large-scale analysis must be built from our understanding of the micropolitics of power at the local level. For him, any attempt to describe power at the level of the state or institution requires us to

> conduct an ascending analysis of power, starting . . . from its infinitesimal mechanisms, which each have their own history, their own trajectory, their own techniques and tactics, and then see how these mechanisms of power have been—and continue to be—invested, colonized, utilized, involuted, transformed, displaced, extended, etc., by ever more general mechanisms and by forms of global domination. (p. 159)

If we accept Foucault's analysis, then many negative features of society are intimately related to the ways in which people organize and act out their everyday lives. Feelings of alienation, stress, and oppression are as much products of everyday, taken-for-granted ways of defining reality and enacting social life as they are the products of systems that are out of people's control. The means by which people are subjugated is to be found in the very "codes" and "discourses" used to organize and enact their day-to-day lives. Oppressive systems of domination and control are maintained not by autocratic processes but through the unconsciously accepted routine practices people use in their families, communities, and occupations.

Foucault suggests that the only way to eliminate this fascism in our heads is to explore and build on the open qualities of human discourse and, thereby, intervene in the way knowledge is constituted at the particular sites where a localized power-discourse prevails. He is concerned that people should cultivate and enhance planning and decision making at the local level, resisting techniques and practices that are oppressive in one way or another. Foucault (1984) instructs us to "develop action, thought and desires by proliferation, juxtaposition, and disjunction," and "to prefer what is positive and multiple, difference over uniformity, flows over unities, mobile arrangements over systems. Believe that what is productive is not sedentary but nomadic" (p. xiii). He suggests, in these words, that we become more flexible in the ways we conceive and organize our activities to ensure that we incorporate diverse perspectives into our social and organizational lives.

The theme of control is also taken up by Fish (1980), who describes social life as "interpretive communities" made up of producers and consumers of particular types of knowledge or "texts." Within these communities, individuals or groups in positions of authority control what they consider to be valid knowledge. Classroom teachers, administrators, managers, social workers, health professionals, administrators, policymakers, and researchers are examples of "producers" who control the texts of social life in their professional domains. In organizing classrooms, writing curricula, defining the rules and procedures by which services operate, formulating policies, and so on, they control the boundaries within which particular interpretive communities will operate. They have the power to dominate the ways in which things happen in their particular domains.

Fish's position is complemented by the work of Lyotard (1984), who casts doubt on the possibility of defining social and organizational life according to well-ordered, logical, and objective (read "scientific") systems of knowledge. He suggests that people live at the intersection of an indeterminate number of language games that, in their entirety, do not constitute a coherent or rational order, although each game operates under a logical set of rules. His vision of a social world atomized into flexible networks of language games suggests that each of us uses a number of different games or codes depending on the context in which we are operating at any given time. There is a contradiction, Lyotard suggests, between the natural openness of social life and the rigidities with which institutions attempt to circumscribe what is and is not admissible within their boundaries.

Derrida's (1976) notion of the interweaving of discourses provides yet another perspective on the texts of social life. Derrida provides insight into why there is a continuing tension between people in positions of control and their subordinates and clients. For him, cultural life can be viewed as series of texts that intersect with other texts through the processes of social interaction. In portraying written texts as cultural artifacts—that is, as human productions—Derrida suggests that both reader and writer interact on the basis of all that they have previously encountered. Both author and reader participate separately in the production of meanings that are inscribed in and derived from that text, although neither can "master" the text—that is, control the meanings conveyed or received—in any ultimate sense. Writers tend to accept the authority to present reality or meaning in their own terms, but these meanings are deconstructed and reconstituted by readers according to their own experiences and interpretive frameworks.

In the context of organizational and institutional life, people such as administrators, teachers, social workers, and other practitioners who control the rules and procedures by which their subordinates, students, or clients work or live often fail to understand that each of the participants will understand those different texts according to his or her own framework of understanding. Even when participants accept what is said or written, they may enact their interpretations of the text in ways that seem to conflict with the perspectives of the authors of the text. Much of the apparent recalcitrance or wrongheadedness of workers, students, and clients might be understood as merely misinterpretation.

There is an implicit ideological position in Derrida's writing. He suggests the need to find new ways of writing texts—rules, procedures, regulations, forms of organization, reports, plans, and so on—to minimize the power of people in positions of authority to impose their perceptions and interpretations. Thus he implies the need to structure organizations in ways that create greater opportunities for popular participation and a more democratic determination of the cultural values embedded in the procedures that govern people's lives. This also implies the need to enact knowledge-producing activities in ways that are more participatory and democratic, enabling the perspectives and agendas of client groups and students to be included in the development of programs that serve them.

Huyssens (1986) is yet another writer who speaks to these issues. He is critical of writers whose theorizing—systems of explanation—presumes to speak for others. He suggests that all groups have the right to speak for themselves, in their own voices, and to have those voices accepted as authentic and legitimate. The authenticity of these "other worlds" and "other voices" is an essential characteristic of the pluralistic stance of many postmodern writers. Huyssens's position has much in common with those of writers such as West (1989) and Unger (1987), who place a premium on the need to educate and be educated by struggling peoples. This stance reflects a movement within the postmodern tradition that shifts the focus of scholarship away from the "search for foundations and the quest for certainty" (West, 1989, p. 213) toward more utilitarian approaches to the production of knowledge.

West (1989) provides a compelling argument for a more pragmatic approach to our ways of understanding the social world. His notion of *prophetic pragmatism* points to the need for an explicitly political mode of cultural criticism. He suggests that philosophy—more generally, intellectual activity or scholarship—should foster methods of examining ordinary and everyday events that encourage a more creative democracy through critical intelligence and social action. He advocates ways of living and working together that provide greater opportunities for people to participate in activities that affect their lives. He urges philosophers—academics, researchers, experts, and professionals—to give up their search for the foundations of truth and the quest for certainty, to shift their energies to defining the social and communal conditions by which people can communicate more effectively and cooperate in the process of acquiring knowledge and making decisions.

The underlying notion in West's (1989) work is not that philosophy and rational deliberation are irrelevant but that they need to be applied directly to the problems of the people. West's pragmatism reconceptualizes philosophy—and therefore research—"as a form of cultural criticism that attempts to transform linguistic, social, cultural and political traditions for the purposes of increasing the scope of individual development and democratic operation" (p. 230). He advocates fundamental economic, political, cultural, and individual transformation that is guided by the ideals of accountable power, small-scale associations, and individual liberty. This transformation can be attained, he implies, only through the reconstruction of the practices and preconceptions embedded in institutional life. On the political level, West acknowledges the need for solidarity with the "wretched of the earth," so that by educating and being educated by struggling peoples, we will be able to relate the life of the mind to the collective life of the community.

West's emphasis on liberation links him, conceptually, with the German scholar Jürgen Habermas, who, although often not classified as postmodern, has provided important ideas that can assist us in understanding human social life. Habermas (1979) focuses on the need to rethink the cultural milieu in which working-class people attempt to find meaning and satisfactory self-identity. He suggests that we clarify the nature of people's subjection and seek human emancipation from the threats of military conflict and dehumanized bureaucratic domination through more effective mechanisms of reflection and communication. Habermas proposes that the emphasis in institutional and organizational life on the factual, material, technical, and administrative neglects the web of intersubjective relations among people that makes possible freedom, harmony, and mutual dependence. His universal pragmatics attempt to delineate the basic conditions necessary for people to reach an understanding. The goal of "communicative action" is an interaction that terminates in "the intersubjective mutuality of reciprocal understanding, shared knowledge, mutual trust and accord with one another" (p. 3).

The general thrust of the ideas presented above is to question many of the basic assumptions on which modern social life is based. In general, these ideas are in opposition to rigidly defined work practices, hierarchical organizational structures, representation in place of participation, the isolation of sectors of activity based on high degrees of specialization, centralized decision making, and the production of social texts by experts or an organizational elite. Inversely, these perspectives suggest emphasis on the following:

- Popular and vernacular language and its meanings
- Pluralistic, organic strategies for development
- The coexistence and interpenetration of meaning systems
- The authenticity of "other worlds" and "other voices"
- Preference for what is multiple, for difference
- Flexibility and mobility of organizational arrangements
- Local creation of texts, techniques, and practices
- Production of knowledge through open discourses
- Flexibility in defining the work people will do
- Restructuring of relations of authority

Postmodern thought moves us, therefore, to examine the ordinary, everyday, taken-for-granted ways in which we organize and carry out our private, social, and professional activities. In the context of this book, it demands that we critically inspect the routines and recipes that have become accepted and commonplace ways of carrying out our professional, organizational, and institutional functions. By illuminating fundamental features of social life, postmodern writers provide us with an opportunity to explore social dimensions of our work and to think creatively about the possibilities for re-creating our professional lives.

The Next Generation:
Community-Based Action Research

This chapter has focused largely on the philosophical foundations of community-based action research. I have presented arguments that seek to substantiate my assertion that it is a legitimate approach to research, despite procedures that vary from commonly accepted practices associated with scientific method. My intent has been not to show that scientific method is wrong or incorrect but to demonstrate that it sits alongside community-based action research as one of a variety of authentic approaches to inquiry.

Even within action research, there is a place for some of the methods, procedures, and concepts usually associated with traditional science. Insofar as people live in a physical universe, traditional scientific research methods—sometimes erroneously labeled *quantitative* research—can provide much useful information. We can describe, for instance, the number of people involved in a setting and how they are distributed geographically, organizationally, and culturally. We can also enumerate the number and proportion of unemployed people, the number and types of dwellings, the age distribution of the population, and relationships that exist among such features as gender, social class, race, educational attainment, employment, and poverty.

The meaning or significance of any of this information, however, can be determined only by the people who live the culture of the setting, who have the profound understanding that comes from extended immersion in the social and cultural life of that context. Numbers can never tell us what the information "means" or suggest actions to be taken.

I was recently engaged in a conversation with a colleague regarding the utility of "counting" events. "Jim," I said, "if, over a period of 6 weeks, I read a local newspaper 40 times, have 120 meals, drink 30 bottles of beer, teach 24 classes, and punch the dean once, which event do you think will be most significant?" In this instance, it is easy to imagine which event is symbolically the most important. In many situations, however, outsiders, expert or otherwise, face grave risks in making judgments about the significance of events. Certainly, the number of times an event occurs is a poor indicator of its symbolic importance or the impact it is likely to have on people's lives.

Community-based action research, therefore, is ultimately a search for meaning. It provides a process or a context through which people can collectively clarify their problems and formulate new ways of envisioning their situations. In doing so, each participant's taken-for-granted cultural viewpoint is challenged and modified so that new systems of meaning emerge that can be incorporated in the texts—rules, regulations, practices, procedures, and policies—that govern our professional and community experience. We come closer to the reality of other people's experience and, in the process, increase the potential for creating truly effective services and programs that will enhance the lives of the people we serve.

This move to emphasize the perspectives and agendas of the client group rather than those of professional practitioners in the development and improvement of programs and services does not mean that simplistic, populist ideas current in mass culture provide the basis for service delivery or institutional practice. The McDonald's Fast-Food Curriculum Model, for instance, might provide a rather unhealthy educational diet in schools. It does mean, however, that professionals take seriously the ideas and perspectives of those they serve, developing ways of working that implicitly honor the intelligence and integrity of the people with whom they work.

Recent theoretical debates have provided substantial recognition of the philosophical strength of this approach to inquiry. The working principles and values revealed in the first chapters of this book are given credence by Denzin's (1997) forward-thinking work, aptly subtitled *Ethnographic Practice for the 21st Century*. He seeks to engage social scientific practices that "will move closer to a sacred, critically informed discourse about the moral, human universe" (p. xviii). Drawing from the work of Christians, Ferre, and Fackler (1993) and Lincoln (1995), he advocates approaches to inquiry that engage a feminist, communitarian moral ethic organized by the following assumptions:

- Community as ontologically and morally superior to persons
- Dialogical communication as the basis for moral community
- Transformation as the major goal of any ethical or occupational practice
- Commitment to the common good and to universal human solidarity

- A sacred conception of science that honors the ecological as well as the human
- A stress on human dignity, care, justice, and interpersonal respect
- Those studied are active participants in collaborative research processes, with claims over any research materials produced in the research process

This model is based on an ethic of caring (Collins, 1991) that celebrates personal expressiveness, emotionality, and empathy; values individual uniqueness; and cherishes each person's dignity, grace, and courage. It is a model, in other words, that fits the intent and processes of community-based action research. It emerges, philosophically, from *standpoint epistemologies*, that is, the ways of knowing and understanding implicit in the experience of particular social groups, that challenge traditional approaches to social science. Standpoint epistemologies emerge from feminist theory contending that studies involving women should privilege women's lived experience and the standpoints, or perspectives, that experience brings to the ethnographic project. These perspectives challenge the notion of a single standpoint from which a final, overriding version of the world can be written (Smith, 1989) and therefore question the ways traditional, patriarchal social science has been constructed. This dynamic extends to other interpretive communities and suggests that ethnic groups, people of color, gays, and so on draw on their group and individual experiences as the basis for texts that speak to the logic and cultures of these communities (Denzin, 1997).

Standpoint perspectives, therefore, advocate ways of formulating reports from the starting point of people's experience to provide a more accurate representation of reality, the production of local knowledge about the workings of the world (Denzin, 1989). Standpoint perspectives suggest the need to recover and bring value to knowledge suppressed by the existing texts and discourses of social science and by interpretations of people's lives that are inscribed in the apparatuses of the state, mass culture, and the popular media.

Patricia Hill Collins's (1991) Afrocentric feminist epistemology, for instance, focuses on the primacy of concrete, lived experience; the use of dialogue in assessing knowledge claims; the ethic of caring; and the ethic of personal accountability. "This epistemology creates the conditions for an existential politics of empowerment that will allow African American women to actively confront racial, gender and class oppression in their daily lives" (p. 237). Trinh (1992) writes from an Asian perspective, challenging systems of domination that seek to impose an essential identity on a person and her experience. She advocates the production of texts that allow women to experience and assert their difference in relation to others and to assume the position of active speakers, listeners, readers, writers, and viewers.

Although standpoint perspectives relate particularly to the experience of marginalized groups, there is a more general point. They should sensitize writers to the need to resist impulses to formulate objective, generalizable accounts claiming to include the perspectives of all people. Reports need to incorporate and represent the perspectives and experiences of the diverse social groups affected by the events and phenomena studied to ensure that the standpoint of each group is presented as authentic and legitimate, rather than an aberration from an hypothetical norm.

Not so long ago, the human services agency in my state produced a carefully compiled child protection manual, complete with detailed procedures for evaluating events related to the well-being of children and formulating appropriate intervention strategies. A consultant had carefully prepared the manual, taking into account the latest information on child protection available in the literature and using intervention strategies that were deemed to be appropriate. The procedures, however, were inappropriate to the realities of Aboriginal family and community life, applying criteria for child care that were contrary to the values and conventions of Aboriginal communities and advocating interventions that were reminiscent of more repressive eras in Aboriginal history. Aboriginal staff of the agency went on strike in one region, forcing the agency to have the offending manual reviewed and modified to take Aboriginal cultural values into account.

Giving Voice:
Representing People's Experience

The desire to give voice to people is derived not from an abstract ideological or theoretical imperative but from the pragmatic focus of action research. Its intent is to provide a place for the perspectives of people who have previously been marginalized from opportunities to develop and operate policies, programs, and services—perspectives often concealed by the products of a typical research process. Research reports often mirror the style of "objective" scientific reports, providing dry, abstract renderings of ideas and events and masking that they are the productions of a socially situated author who writes from his or her own history of experience. The process often encapsulates events within the mystifying jargon of academic disciplines or buries them in the conceptual apparatuses of a bureaucracy.

Previous sections of this book have suggested alternative ways for community-based action research participants to represent more effectively the outcomes of their research processes. The purpose of these alternatives is to ensure that accounts and reports capture the people's everyday, concrete, human experiences, allowing audiences to understand more clearly the realities of people's lives. The need for changes in reporting procedures is clearly presented in an increasing body of research literature (e.g., Berger Gluck & Patai, 1991; Bruner, 1990; Burnaford, Fischer, & Hobson, 1996; Lincoln & Tierney, 1996; Neumann & Peterson, 1997; Witherall & Noddings, 1991). These and many other authors explore ways of representing people's experience to more effectively grasp the many dimensions of life that formal, official reports often fail to reveal.

Denzin (1997) explores the underlying assumptions and principles of ethnographic writing and many of the dimensions of the reporting act. In so doing, he suggests that authors of official and academic reports might usefully employ technical processes used by journalists and fiction writers. He starts from the assumption that it is impossible to write objective accounts not ultimately inscribed with the perspectives and experiences of the author because of the interpretive processes inherent in data collection, analysis, and report writing. Drawing on a wide range of authors, he suggests that experiments in genre, voice, narrative, and interpretive style will provide more effective ways of knowing, other ways of feeling our way into the experiences of others. Such writing, he suggests, will reveal the meaning of events given by interacting individuals, focusing on experience that is deeply embedded in and derived from local cultural contexts—contexts that will include homes, offices, schools, streets, factories, clinics, hotels, and so on. These accounts and reports will recognize and represent the multiple interpretations of any event or phenomenon yet also acknowledge the broader discourses that are inscribed or imprinted in people's local experiences—government policies, incipient racism, systems of privilege, imbalances of power based on social status, and so on.

Denzin works from the premise that the purpose of accounts derived from research processes is more than to record experience. Their goal, rather, is to provide the basis for transforming people's civic, public, and personal lives through the truths, the new ways of describing and interpreting events, revealed in the research process. Reports, therefore, must be more than impersonal, abstract accounts of "facts," which themselves are merely pieces of information acquired and interpreted selectively. They must be empathetic, evocative accounts that embody the significant experiences embedded in the taken-for-granted world of people's everyday lives. They must record the agonies, pains, tragedies, triumphs, actions, behaviors, and deeply felt emotions—love, pride, dignity, honor, hate, and envy—that constitute the real world of human experience.

In this context, the researcher-writer takes a different stance in the research and writing process. No longer "experts" capable of defining, describing, and interpreting the "facts" or "truth," researcher-writers position themselves quite differently. They move toward writing processes that assist others in describing and interpreting their own experiences, sometimes acting as scribes for research participants or as coauthors or editors. The writer as scribe-for-the-other helps people give voice to their own interpretations of events, working with them to identify the key elements of their experience and shape them into a report.

Practice Scripts:
Policies, Plans, and Procedures

Change is an intended outcome of community-based action research: not the revolutionary changes envisioned by radical social theorists or political activists, but more subtle transformations brought about by the development of new programs or modifications to existing procedures. These developments and modifications, however, must necessarily be carefully planned and derived from the research processes to provide people with the means to more effectively deal with the problems investigated. The procedures presented in Chapters 6 and 7 suggest some ways of moving from reflection and theorizing to action. These moves need to be made more explicit so that the institutional imperatives of universities and bureaucracies do not inhibit the potential of the research process. There is a need to more overtly review the outcomes of research so that they are presented in forms that may be applied directly to the texts that govern much institutional life: the policies, plans, and procedures that dictate how programs and services are delivered to the people served by those institutions.

Experiments with forms of writing that more effectively capture people's experience, discussed in the previous section, are moves in the right direction, but they appear limited in their ability to provide tangible outcomes for those who participate in research. Academic research tends to focus on the production of written texts that reflect the imperatives of university life, and research reports often remain trapped within the walls of the university. They circulate within the texts and journals of the university and, even when enacted as performances, are presented as theatrical productions playing to audiences oriented toward institutional life. They do not penetrate the everyday life-world of homes, schools, clinics, offices, shops, and factories and are especially remote from marginalized peoples whose lives are often framed by oral traditions that are misrepresented by the forms of understanding presented in written texts.

Even approaches to research designed to be more sensitive to these dynamics are prone to processes of knowledge production that colonize the experience of others. Denzin's (1997) interpretive ethnography, for instance, seeks to produce evocative understandings through a variety of literary forms that perform or write of people's experience (see Chapter 5). Research products, such as reports, presentations, and performances, are taken from the locations of the study and used as generalized narratives for an audience unrelated to the research context. Those texts and performances largely are used by others to enable them to understand the experience of those written about and to place that experience in an etic (outsider) framework of generalized theory. Such theorizing tends to be macrofocused, incorporating broad concepts, such as power, class, gender, race, and so on, often providing no basis for action in people's daily lives. The terminology turns the focus away from people's lived experience toward more general social processes that they have little opportunity or hope of controlling. Critiques within this type of literary production usually focus on negative constructions of the situation, often framed within descriptions and explanations of macrosocial and cultural structures and treated as real entities, rather than as constructed ways of interpreting social phenomena.

These texts and performances are sometimes illuminating activities that provide understanding of the broader contexts within which people's lives are played out, revealing underlying forces of social life that are not evident existentially. They are, however, etic (outsider) constructs that have the power to distort people's lived reality and misrepresent the existential experience of their everyday lives. They tend to be generalizing interpretations that focus on underlying elements of social life such as power, race, and gender rather than revealing the dynamic, interactive play of people and events as they work their way through their day-to-day lives. Dealing with macrostructures as they do, they often fail to provide the possibility for restorative action and run the risk, therefore, of becoming voyeuristic and disempowering.

The use of those types of production should, perhaps, not be underestimated because they do provide useful ways of communicating evocative interpretations of social life that inform readers of social realities far removed from their own experiences. Community-based action research, however, suggests the possibility of more socially responsive uses of research, providing the means for people to have a more direct impact on the significant issues that continue to detract from their social life and to make a tangible difference to the problems that diminish their lives. It reconceptualizes research as a participatory process that allows scholars—to follow West's (1989) dictum—to make their skills available for the purposes of the people.

Community-based action research enacts localized, pragmatic approaches to research, investigating particular issues and problems in particular sites, at particular moments in lives of interacting individuals and groups. Its purpose is to provide participants with new understandings of an issue they have defined as significant and the means for taking corrective action. The processes are necessarily participatory, enabling all people affected by the issue to have their voices heard and to be actively engaged in research activities. Community-based action research suggests a move in emphasis from the creative texts of experimental interpretive ethnography toward the production of *practice scripts*. Practice scripts are the plans, procedures, and models derived from the final stages of action research that enable people to take direct action on the problems they have investigated. They also provide the means for people in professional or occupational roles to reformulate policies and practices to enable them to provide programs and services that are more effective (see Box 9.1).

Although academic research often seeks critique from within the constructs of the social sciences, critique in community-based action research derives from the conjunction/clash of the diverse perspectives of individuals and groups participating, each perspective being challenged by the others. Critique is derived not from an etic, outsider interpretive framework but from the process of exploring and negotiating the different perspectives emerging from the process of investigation. It uses concepts and terms from within the context, rather than those drawn from academic texts or bureaucratic discourses, and seeks constructions and interpretations of the issue that provide the basis for direct, tangible uses within the research context.

Change, the desired outcome of community-based action research, therefore derives from the here-and-now ideas and concepts taken from the taken-for-granted life-world of the participants. It is based on the language, ideas, and concepts that "make sense" in their homes, offices, schools, factories, shops, clinics, centers, organizations, and institutions and are part of their everyday experience of family, community, work, professional, and commercial life. The products of research are not only written reports but also *practice scripts*—plans, procedures, models,

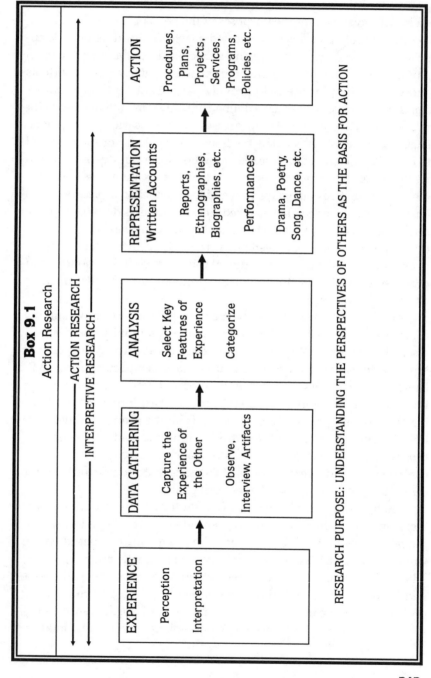

Box 9.1

Action Research

EXPERIENCE

Perception

Interpretation

DATA GATHERING

Capture the
Experience of
the Other

Observe,
Interview, Artifacts

ANALYSIS

Select Key
Features of
Experience

Categorize

REPRESENTATION

Written Accounts

Reports,
Ethnographies,
Biographies, etc.

Performances

Drama, Poetry,
Song, Dance, etc.

ACTION

Procedures,
Plans,
Projects,
Services,
Programs,
Policies, etc.

◀——— ACTION RESEARCH ———▶

◀——— INTERPRETIVE RESEARCH

RESEARCH PURPOSE: UNDERSTANDING THE PERSPECTIVES OF OTHERS AS THE BASIS FOR ACTION maps, and so on—that provide the basis for reformulating practices, policies, programs, and services related to people's occupational or community life.

I am reminded of the long list of official policies, projects, programs, and institutional processes that have damaged the lives of minority peoples in Australia and the United States. I think of Dee Brown's *Bury My Heart at Wounded Knee* (1970) and Anna Haebich's *For Their Own Good* (1988), both of which depict the disastrous impacts of official policies on the lives of indigenous peoples. I think of the way that I organized my classroom in an Aboriginal school, so that children were forced to sit with others with whom they had a taboo or avoidance relationship. I think of academics who, from the safety of their ivory tower, formulate research projects that are implicitly critical of professional practitioners. The list goes on. Last night, a good friend and I, musing over these dynamics, thought of the old saying that "the road to hell is paved with good intentions."

But I am also reminded of the great triumphs of those who worked with people so that they became the instruments of their own liberation. Great leaders such as Mohandas Gandhi and Martin Luther King, Jr., come to mind, but I am conscious of a flood of other local heroes with smaller accomplishments: the woman who established a play group to help young mothers come together to discuss their common issues—the genesis of a widespread network of play groups in my own state—and the psychiatrist who worked with parents and students in her local community to establish an independent school as a haven from a school ruled by an authoritarian principal. Fortunately, that list also goes on.

In the Company of Friends

In this chapter, I have spoken of the dimension of power in community-based research. For some, the move to empower people is seen as divisive, confrontational interactions and activities that enable one person or group to wrest control from another. The communitarian ethic embedded in community-based action research, however, suggests a more consensual approach to investigation requiring participants to enact the working principles discussed in Chapter 2. The position of the researcher changes from one of controller, advocate, or activist to one of facilitator. The researcher's role is not to push particular agendas but to neutralize power differentials in the setting so that the interests of the powerful do not take precedence over those of other participants. Interactions and activities must, however, allay the fears of people in positions of power, generating levels of trust that enable them to feel sufficiently at ease to release some of their control over events. Their acquiescence is an essential feature of community-based action research. They should feel that their institutional or organizational responsibilities, or their place and status in the context, are not threatened by the research activities.

Procedures must also generate trust within less powerful groups, so that they are willing to participate in arenas in which previously they have been mistreated or demeaned. The reward for both types of groups is that they acquire ends or goals that otherwise would not have been possible for either, working by themselves.

The power broker role of the researcher is exercised with the intent of facilitating change in the power dynamics of the situation. The result is not so much a transfer of power from one group to another—although that often occurs—as a change in the *nature* of power relations. Power is still exercised, but in a different way. A teacher in a classroom does not relinquish the responsibility of facilitating students' education. The teacher can, however, choose to provide significant decision-making opportunities to students regarding the organization of the class, the curriculum, the timetable, and so on. Social workers and health professionals may similarly engage client groups in the process of formulating or restructuring the ways in which programs and services are organized and administered.

Improved service delivery and problem resolution are not the only goals of these types of activities. Community-based action research seeks to formulate ways of living and working together that will enhance the life experiences of the participants. It provides ways of working that counter the impact of the current overemphasis on the technical and the bureaucratic and enables the formulation of procedures that take into account those features of a situation that are essentially human—that speak to issues of emotion, value, and identity.

Ultimately, however, the routines of community-based action research suggest ways of working that enable a harmonious and productive sense of social life. The end product is, if anything, peace of mind or the chance to participate in the pursuit of happiness. It is a movement away from competitive, power-driven, conflict-ridden organizational processes toward more cooperative, consensual ways of living.

A colleague once suggested that education could be defined as "the search for truth in the company of friends." Although "truth" may elude us, community-based action research might, in a similar vein, be defined as "the search for understanding in the company of friends."

Appendix

Action Research Electronic Resources

An increasing body of action research resources is available on the Internet. The following list is far from exhaustive but provides a way of entering this electronic world. The names and places give some indication of the focus of the resource and the particular emphasis of the address:

Action Research List (Bob Dick, Southern Cross University)

```
ftp://psych.psy.uq.oz.au/lists/arlist/ar_arlist
```

Associated resources:

```
ftp://psych.psy.uq.oz.au/lists/arlist/ar_biblio (Action
Research Bibliography)
```

```
http://elmo.scu.edu.au/schools/sawd/ari/ar.html (Action
Research Resources)
```

Action Research On the Web Help (Geoff Mills, Southern Oregon University)

   http://beta.open.k12.or.us/dennis/arowhelp/index.html

Community Action Research Network (University of East Anglia)

   http://www.uea.ac.uk/care/carn/

Centre for Action Research in Professional Practice (Peter Reason, University of Bath)

   http://www.bath.ac.uk/carpp

Jack Whitehead's Home Page (University of Bath)

   http://www.bath.ac.uk/edsajw/

Participatory Action Research Network (Carla Shafer, Cornell University)

   http://www.parnet.org/home.cfmPARnet

Web Links to Participatory Action Research Sites (Gosham College)

   http://www.goshen.edu/soan/soan96p.htm

References

Anderson, G., Herr, K., & Nihlen, A. (1994). *Studying your own school: An educator's guide to qualitative practitioner research.* Thousand Oaks, CA: Corwin.

Atweh, B., Weeks, P., & Kemmis, S. (Eds.). (1998). *Action research in practice: Partnerships for social justice in education.* New York: Routledge.

Berger Gluck, S., & Patai, D. (Eds.). (1991). *Women's words: The feminist practice of oral history.* New York: Routledge.

Black, J. P. (1991). *Development in theory and practice: Bridging the gap.* Boulder, CO: Westview.

Block, P. (1990). *The empowered manager: Positive political skills at work.* San Francisco: Jossey-Bass.

Boyarsky, N., & Murphy, N. (1998). *Action research* (Black dog series, Vol. 1). N.p.: Art Books International.

Brown, A., & Dowling, P. (1998). *Doing research/reading research: A mode of interrogation for education.* London: Falmer.

Brown, D. (1970). *Bury my heart at Wounded Knee: An Indian history of the American west.* London: Vintage.

Bruner, J. (1990). *Acts of meaning.* Cambridge, MA: Harvard University Press.

Burnaford, G., Fischer, J., & Hobson, D. (Eds.). (1996). *Teachers doing research: Practical possibilities.* Mahwah, NJ: Lawrence Erlbaum.

Calhoun, E. (1993, October). Action research: Three approaches. *Educational Leadership, 51*(2), 62-65.

Carr, W., & Kemmis, S. (1986). *Becoming critical: Education, knowledge, and action research.* Philadelphia: Falmer.

Christians, C., Ferre, J., & Fackler, M. (1993). *Good news: Social ethics and the press.* New York: Oxford University Press.

Christiansen, H., Goulet, L., Krentz, C., & Maeers, M. (Eds.). (1997). *Recreating relationships: Collaboration and educational reform.* Albany: State University of New York Press.

Collins, P. (1991). *Black feminist thought.* New York: Routledge.

Coover, V., Deacon, E., Esser, C., & Moore, C. (1985). *Resource manual for a living revolution.* Philadelphia: New Society.

Denzin, N. K. (1989). *Interpretive interactionism.* Newbury Park, CA: Sage.

Denzin, N. K. (1997). *Interpretive ethnography.* Thousand Oaks, CA: Sage.

Denzin, N. K., & Lincoln, Y. S. (Eds.). (1994). *Handbook of qualitative research.* Thousand Oaks, CA: Sage.

Derrida, J. (1976). *Of grammatology.* Baltimore, MD: Johns Hopkins University Press.

Deshler, D. (1990). Conceptual mapping: Drawing charts of the mind. In J. Mezirow & Associates (Eds.), *Fostering critical reflection in adulthood* (pp. 336-353). San Francisco: Jossey-Bass.

Fals-Borda, O., & Rahman, M. (Eds.). (1991). *Action and knowledge: Breaking the monopoly with participatory action-research.* New York: Apex.

Fish, S. (1980). *Is there a text in this class? The authority of interpretive communities.* Cambridge, MA: Harvard University Press.

Foucault, M. (1972). *The archaeology of knowledge.* New York: Random House.

Foucault, M. (1979). *Discipline and punish: The birth of the prison.* New York: Vintage.

Foucault, M. (1984). *The Foucault reader* (P. Rabinow, Ed.). Harmondsworth, UK: Penguin.

Freire, P. (1974). *Pedagogy of the oppressed.* New York: Seabury.

Gastil, J. (1993). *Democracy in small groups: Participation, decision making, and communication.* Philadelphia: New Society.

Genat, W. (1998). *Aboriginal health workers: Beyond the clinic, beyond the rhetoric.* Unpublished manuscript, Perth, Western Australia.

Goodenough, W. (1963). *Cooperation in change: An anthropological approach to community development.* New York: Russell Sage.

Greenwood, D., & Levin, M. (1998). *Introduction to action research: Social research for social change.* Thousand Oaks, CA: Sage.

Guba, E. G. (1990). *The paradigm dialogue.* Newbury Park, CA: Sage.

Guba, E. G., & Lincoln, Y. S. (1989). *Fourth generation evaluation.* Newbury Park, CA: Sage.

Habermas, J. (1979). *Communication and the evolution of society* (T. McCarthy, Trans.). Boston: Beacon.

Haebich, A. (1988). *For their own good.* Perth: University of Western Australia Press.

Hart, E., & Bond, M. (1995). *Action research for health and social care: A guide to practice.* London: Open University Press.

Huyssens, A. (1986). *After the great divide: Modernism, mass culture, postmodernism.* Bloomington: Indiana University Press.

Kelly, A., & Gluck, R. (1979). *Northern Territory community development.* Unpublished manuscript, University of Queensland, St. Lucia, Australia.

Kelly, A., & Sewell, S. (1988). *With head, heart, and hand.* Brisbane, Queensland, Australia: Boolarong.

Kemmis, S., & McTaggart, R. (1988). *The action research planner.* Geelong, Victoria, Australia: Deakin University Press.

Kickett, D., McCauley, D., & Stringer, E. (1986). *Community development processes: An introductory handbook.* Perth, Western Australia: Curtin University of Technology.

Kincheloe, J. (1991). *Teachers as researchers: Qualitative inquiry as a path to empowerment.* London: Falmer.

Krulfeld, R., MacDonald, J. R., & MacDonald, J. L. (Eds.). (1998). *Power, ethics, and human rights: Anthropological studies of refugee research and action.* Savage, MD: Rowman & Littlefield.

Lewin, K. (1946). Action research and minority problems. *Journal of Social Issues, 2,* 34-46.

Lincoln, Y. S. (1995). Emerging criteria for quality in qualitative and interpretive inquiry. *Qualitative Inquiry, 1,* 275-289.

Lincoln, Y. S., & Guba, E. G. (1985). *Naturalistic inquiry.* Beverly Hills, CA: Sage.

Lincoln, Y. S., & Tierney, W. (1996). *Representation and the text: Reframing the narrative voice.* Albany: State University of New York Press.

Lyotard, J.-F. (1984). *The postmodern condition: A report on knowledge.* Minneapolis: University of Minnesota Press.

Malinowski, B. (1961). *Argonauts of the western Pacific: An account of native enterprise and adventure in the archipelagoes of Melanesian New Guinea.* New York: E. P. Dutton. (Original work published 1922)

McCauley, D. (1985). *Community development.* Unpublished manuscript, Perth, Western Australia.

McNiff, J. (1995). *Action research principles and practice.* New York: Routledge.

McTaggart, R. (Ed.). (1997). *Participatory action research: International contexts and consequences.* Albany: State University of New York Press.

Mead, G. H. (1934). *Mind, self, and society: From the standpoint of a social behaviorist.* Chicago: University of Chicago Press.

Mills, G. (in press). *Action research: A guide for the teacher researcher.* Columbus, OH: Merrill/Prentice Hall.

Moreno, J. (1956). *Sociometry and the science of man.* New York: Beacon.

Mumford, A. (Ed.). (1997). *Action learning at work.* Aldershot, UK: Gower.

Neumann, A., & Peterson, P. (1997). *Women, research, and autobiography in education.* New York: Teachers College Press.

Peck, M. S. (1993). *A world waiting to be born: Civility rediscovered.* New York: Bantam.

Reason, P. (1994). Three approaches to participative inquiry. In N. K. Denzin & Y. S. Lincoln (Eds.), *Handbook of qualitative research* (pp. 324-339). Thousand Oaks, CA: Sage.

Reason, P. (Ed.). (1988). *Human inquiry in action: Developments in new paradigm research.* Newbury Park, CA: Sage.

Reason, P., & Rowan, J. (Eds.). (1981). *Human inquiry: A sourcebook of new paradigm research.* New York: John Wiley.

Schmuck, R. (1998). *Practical action research for change.* Boston: Allyn & Bacon.

Smith, D. E. (1989). Sociological theory: Methods of writing patriarchy. In R. A. Wallace (Ed.), *Feminism and sociological theory* (pp. 34-64). Newbury Park, CA: Sage.

Spradley, J. P. (1979). *The ethnographic interview.* New York: Holt, Rinehart & Winston.

Stringer, E. (1997). *Community based ethnography: Breaking traditional boundaries of research, teaching and learning.* Mahwah, NJ: Lawrence Erlbaum.

Trinh, M.-H. (1992). *Framer framed.* New York: Routledge.

Unger, R. (1987). *Social theory, its situation and its task.* Cambridge, UK: Cambridge University Press.

Van Willigen, J. (1993). *Applied anthropology.* South Hadley, MA: Bergin & Garvey.

Vlachos, E. (1975). *Social impact assessment: An overview.* Fort Belvoir, VA: Army Corps of Engineers, Institute of Water Resources.

Wadsworth, Y. (1997). *Everyday evaluation on the run* (2nd ed.). St. Leonards, New South Wales, Australia: Allen & Unwin.

Wallace, M. (1998). *Action research for language teachers.* Cambridge, UK: Cambridge University Press.

Weisbrod, B., & Worthy, J. (Eds.). (1997). *The urban crisis: Linking research to action.* Evanston, IL: Northwestern University Press.

West, C. (1989). *The American evasion of philosophy.* Madison: University of Wisconsin Press.

Whyte, W. F. (1984). *Learning from the field: A guide from experience.* Beverly Hills, CA: Sage.

Witherall, C., & Noddings, N. (Eds.). (1991). *Stories lives tell: Narrative and dialogue in education.* New York: Teachers College Press.

Index

223

About the Author

Ernest T. Stringer has a B.A. and a B.Ed. from the University of Western Australia and an A.M. and a Ph.D. from the University of Illinois at Champaign-Urbana. His early work as primary teacher and school principal in Western Australia and Britain was complemented by work in teacher education programs at Curtin University of Technology in Western Australia. Since 1983, he has worked in the Centre for Aboriginal Studies at Curtin University, where, in conjunction with Aboriginal staff and community people, he has participated in the development of a variety of education and community development programs and services and where he is currently engaged in teaching postgraduate programs. More recently, as Visiting Associate Professor at Texas A&M University and the University of New Mexico, he has extended his interests in sociology, anthropology, and philosophy through explorations of postmodern social theory and naturalistic and interpretive research methods. The outcomes have become incorporated into the collaborative, participatory, and community-based approaches to teaching and research that now form the basis for much of his work.